YOU ARE THE KEY

A GUIDE TO
SELF-DISCOVERY

SHAUN DE WARREN

*"The single most important work we can
be engaged in is to work on ourselves"*

WELLSPRING PUBLICATIONS LIMITED
46 Cyril Mansions, Prince of Wales Drive
London SW11 4HW, England

YOU ARE THE KEY—A Guide to Self-Discovery
2nd Printing 1992

Also from Wellspring

By Shaun de Warren
THE MIRROR OF LIFE—Your Adventure in Self-Discovery

In collaboration with Susan Mayne and Sue Lake
THE 10-DAY BROWN RICE DIET—A Journey Towards Inner
and Outer Wellbeing

Compilations
THE RELATIONSHIPS HANDBOOK—Jewels to Bring Love
and Happiness
THE HEALTH HANDBOOK—Pearls to Inspire Healing
THE PROSPERITY HANDBOOK—Gems to enrich your life
and pocket

*For details of Shaun de Warren's other publications, tapes, lectures, and
workshops, please write to:* WELLSPRING PUBLICATIONS

By Chuck Spezzano, Ph.D.
AWAKEN THE GODS—Aphorisms to Remember the Way Home

ISBN 0 9513520 0 8

Further copies may be obtained from:
Wellspring Publications,
46 Cyril Mansions, Prince of Wales Drive
London SW11 4HW, England

Printed and bound in Great Britain by
BPCC Wheatons Ltd, Exeter

CONTENTS

ACKNOWLEDGEMENTS

My thanks to Denis Vaughan who had the vision of this book and who took copious and brilliant notes at various lectures and meetings and for all of his inspiration and encouragement; to Brian Mayne for his invaluable support and assistance in the preparation and clarification of the notes for publication; to Julian Bradley for his helpful typing and editing; to Denis Vaughan and Sylvia de Warren for proof-reading; to Gill Coupland for the design and production; and to my clients and the members of The Centre in Battersea for creating the space for this book and for drawing from me the thoughts and ideas presented here.

My thanks and acknowledgement also goes to the many people, organisations and teachings that have influenced me and inspired me along the way including Grace, Paul Twitchell and the teachings and leadership of Eckankar, Anne Parks, Ted Long, Werner Erhard and the programmes and leadership of the Centres Network, Douglas Harding, Leonard Orr, Jose Silva, Walter Russell, Lord Exeter and the Emmissary Network, Joan Holmes and the leadership of The Hunger Project, Lionel Fifield, Joel Goldsmith, Nisargadatta, Sri Aurobindo, The Mother, Swami Shyam and the people of the International Meditation Institute in Kullu, India.

INTRODUCTION

I first heard Shaun de Warren speak over ten years ago in Milan, then in Munich. The clarity of his propositions, his compelling use of paradox, and the inevitable feeling of at last having understood something which had irked me for years singled him out as a rare specimen in the greater sea of spiritual advisers. The disciplines of a cavalry officer and a barrister require clear aims, urgency, precision and eloquence. Apply all these attributes to spiritual matters, which are usually greatly resistant to definition, and you can understand why Shaun is emerging as one of the most prophetic voices – dare I say thinkers – in the world.

At a lecture at the Institute for Complementary Medicine, London, Shaun gave a series of precepts for new perspectives; new ways to regard old habits. We were all so impressed that we asked for a list of the precepts. When the following week he came empty-handed, we asked him to repeat the lecture of the previous week. This was the beginning of my jottings, for which I am fundamentally grateful. I found that if you write something down, there is a better chance that you might begin to understand it.

After these notes had been circulated over several months, it was evident that they were very useful to people who had attended the lectures, serving rather as a snapshot to recall a happy event. When the pile had reached twenty, it became clear that a book would be the most useful way to circulate them. We have experimented with layout, and come to the conclusion that the original note-form is the most compelling. Nearly all of the ideas are of equal importance, and they gain the maximum energy when they are put down with the same imperative vigour with which Shaun delivers them.

Each reader will discover his or her favourite method for absorbing these precepts. Perhaps a page at a time, perhaps just a line at a time. One thing is sure: they are not addressed to the logical mind, but to the subconscious. Please don't expect a watertight, philosophical presentation – only a set of ideas which I have found tend to make you feel better the more you become acquainted with them. Each of these precepts means something different to each reader. I am curious to know what you will make of them?

Denis Vaughan

NEW PERSPECTIVES

Twenty-Eight Ways to Escape Mental Traps
or
How to Live in the Now!

1. Heal the past.
    Complete unhealed relationships, incomplete cycles and
        unfulfilled wishes.
    Dissolve regret, guilt and embarrassment.
    Our relationships with parents in particular need healing.
    To heal means returning to wholeness and completeness
        – giving up blame and judgement.

2. Forgive.
    Forgiveness is not to be confused with "the good me
        forgives the bad you", which is not forgiveness at
        all.
    True forgiveness is coming from the place that "nothing
        was ever wrong".
    The essence of all is good.
    Therefore, by returning everything to the whole, belief in
        evil disapppears.
    Seeming negative events are gifts which, with the right
        attitude, can assist you in your personal
        development.
    Release everyone.
    Adopt the attitude that nothing was ever wrong.
    Thus we can heal relationships and avoid being bound by
        other people.

3. Remember I AM.

   The true reality is I AM.

   It is the space where nothing changes and where no
   external influence can have effect – the centre of
   our being

4. Explore the idea that there is only one anything!

   This concept is fundamental.

   There is only Self.

   Mind sees separateness.

   There is only one human being (human beingness) of
   which we are all individual examples.

   With the physical eye we see duality of form.

   With the spiritual eye we see the oneness of all things.

   Self, Mastery, Love, Truth and Life are formless and
   indivisible.

5. Be here.

   To be fully here is to acknowledge all "there" as here
   also.

   "There" disappears as a separate position. Dualities
   disappear.

   Paradoxes disappear.

   "Here" and "there" disappear. "Now" and "then"
   disappear.

   In here and now there is no night and day – only day; no
   life and death – only life; no sickness and health –
   only health.

6. Dissolve form.

   "I am presence."

   Try closing your eyes and experiencing your Being
   beyond form.

   The experience of Being pervades the whole body and is
   felt by the cells as love.

   Attachment to form is a function of the mind.

7. Collapse all duality.

    To collapse duality we must acknowledge ourselves as space, which we feel as beingness.

    Acknowledge the real self as formless.

    Our Self is not external to anything and contains everything.

    "I am space (beingness) and as that I find my true relationship with life."

    Thinking, which is bound to form, severely limits our ability to relate.

8. Expose the only enemy: the one you create in your thinking.

    Heal the world by healing your thinking.

9. Realise that your centre is neutral.

    Nothing has meaning unless you say so.

    You give value to all external reality.

    Things only have the meaning that you give them.

    Explanations and reasons are self-created rationalisations and have no value other than satisfying the mind.

    Do not live in your reasons.

    Have what you want.

    Reasons have no power to create – only Self does.

10. Express only love.

    Love is the basis of all life.

    Unless our life is based in love we are wasting our time.

    Mind is based in fear and desire unless it is aligned with Self.

    Sin is mankind's mental construction designed to stop the free expression of love. It is failing to align ourselves with love as a base.

11. Realise that everyone is whole, complete and perfect.
    The essence of all of us is whole, complete and perfect –
        already now.
    Acknowledging your own divinity leads you to freedom.
    Wrestling with your perceived imperfections does not.
    Don't hold yourself back in imperfection.

12. Align your mind with Source, so that body, mind and self
    become as one.

13. Create your own life.
    See life as your personal training programme.
    It is your own creation and everyone and every event is
        your teacher and mirror.
    They reflect to you your way Home.

14. Let go of judgement.
    "Right and wrong" as a concept is dualistic.
    We make it up ourselves, according to how we feel.
    Let go of your positions and dwell in truth.
    It is sometimes useful to have viewpoints and preferences,
        but do not stand on their "rightness".
    There is no *right*.

15. Use intuition.
    Trust your Self not your mind.
    Intuition is our most powerful guide, more powerful than
        any expert.

16. See only opportunities.
    All problems are opportunities.
    Look out always for the possibilities that problems
        represent.

17. Use the laws of manifestation.

Commit to the results you want.

See the result as a present reality already achieved.

Then lay plans and follow the action indicated by your intuition.

Use the billiard ball technique.

Image the ball already in the pocket and allow intuition to show you how to hit it.

Mind tries to calculate a logical sequence and, as a result, often does not succeed.

18. Tell the truth.

The truth sets you free.

Lies bind.

What is true is what I am experiencing right now.

"You upset me" is a judgement and untrue.

"I feel upset" is an experience and true.

By living in judgement of others, we convince ourselves that what happens to us is the effect, and so we are stuck with our upset.

By being the source of our upset, we can dissolve it.

19. Be a giver.

A getter does not know who he is.

Giving is the natural expression of Self.

The sun only gives.

Giving includes the process of giving and receiving and acknowledges the natural process of circulation.

If you want to receive money, give money. If you want to receive love, give love.

The giving always comes first.

Dwell in the circulation of wealth.

Profusion and abundance are natural conditions.

20. Take responsibility for your life.
  You are the source of all of it.
  Give up blaming others – including God.
  Give up hoping that someone else will do it for you.
  Hope should be totally discarded, because it implies failure.
  No one can or should do it for you anyway.
21. See living life as a game.
  Give up seeing life as struggle and opposition.
  Learn the rules ... and enjoy playing.
22. Choose the way of Self (Oneness) – not the way of mind (twoness).
  Let go.
  Relax all body and mental tension.
23. Live in your vision.
  See the way you want it and live that way.
  Do not try to adjust to the condition in which you find yourself.
24. Expect miracles as a daily occurrence.
25. Be grateful for all things (however good or seemingly bad).
  This clears the Chakras.
26. Give up trying to be better and different.
  Enjoy being yourself.
  Enjoy being united with everyone.
  It is far less stressful.
27. Have a good clean out.
  Baggage is heavy.

28. Nothing happens until you make a commitment with the whole of your body and emotions.
  Really mean and feel what you say.

AWARENESS

Awareness is the foundation of Being.
From awareness we come into consciousness.
Consciousness comes and goes.
Awareness is always present even though we do not perceive it.
In consciousness we tend to associate with the body/mind
   complex whether in "awakeness" or "sleepness".
We must make the fundamental shift from alignment with our
   habitual body/mind complex into the "I AM" of pure
   awareness.
We become aware and conscious of our various levels of
   dreaming.
These include what we usually regard as the "awake" state,
   which is also a level of dreaming.

Growth is not so much expanding our consciousness as learning
   to acknowledge awareness as our ground of Being.
Do not strive or seek for greater consciousness.
Stop seeking and be a finder.
The exploration *starts* from "I AM".
Who I AM is the power and the prosperity.
Take the step backwards into ourselves, into Being, and out of
   the formbound "reality", in order to feel what I AM really
   means.
Living life then becomes the workshop and the adventure.
We look at everything from a new perspective.
In this state of sharpened awareness we are open to and can
   relate to experiences which other people are sharing.
To increase your awareness of what *others* are thinking about,
   increase your awareness of what *you* are thinking.
The more you are aware of yourself and your mental mechanics,
   the easier it is to spot them and the mechanisms of others.

7

Thus, in a group, another person's experience can be the key to heightening our own awareness.

Similarly, when you say "this is what's happening to me", everyone can relate to it.

That is because it is true, and everyone can get a sense of it.

Awareness is a clean canvas.

We are the artist.

What we put on the canvas is what is happening in consciousness.

Once you know that you are the clean canvas, you can put any painting you like on it.

It therefore follows that you have designed the structure of mind through which you are operating.

When we know that we are the artist, creating our own life, what we do is an expression of ourselves and not a needing.

The two barriers to awareness are fear and desire.

We remove these barriers by turning our attention to oneness.

Dwelling in oneness eliminates desire and fear.

So to be totally aware we must let go of any attachment to our body/mind habits.

Moments of pure lucidity are when we are "The Presence".

Being in heaven does not mean that everything is wonderful.

It is merely a context within which we live our lives – life as heaven.

"I live in heaven and live my life accordingly."

The other choice would be "being in hell."

Even with full awareness we may still not feel good.

Awareness means something else – an alertness.

Yet how we feel does not always determine our state of awareness.

The conditions outside us do not determine who we are.

For example, "I am happy, but things are tough" is not a contradiction.

"I am happy" is my ground of Being.

"Things are tough" is the condition.
Our task is to transform our condition (toughness) and raise it
    to our context (happiness).

Soul (or Self) wishes to express itself.
We must align with the Self and allow it to express.
We must always start the process.
This can be done in meditation when the mind operates in the
    Alpha/Theta/Delta levels, stilling the busy butterfly
    activity of the Beta level.
When we feel incomplete, it is only the mind which feels
    incomplete.
Self is complete.
To find the Self, go into meditation , from where the mind
    incompletions can be healed.
Remind yourself that you are love expressing and any feeling of
    incompletion will disappear.
Completion creates space.
The process is space-creation-action-completion-space.
When something is returned to space it is complete.
For something to be complete does not mean it is ended, for it
    can be part of a cycle or of further growth.
It means it is returned to the wholeness, e.g., a complete
    relationship is one which exists within love and freedom.
A person with whom you have a complete relationship may
    only see you once in ten years, but there is always love,
    goodwill and a joy in being together.
You feel complete, as if you were never apart.

See yourself as the whole universe wherever you walk.
Experience the universe walking through you.
Make the basic shift from "it is all happening over there"
    (formbound reality) to "it is all happening here in me"
    (operation from space).
This is the perspective of oneness.
In oneness we Know.

9

THE ART OF GIVING

Giving and taking are opposites.
Giving and receiving are a function of Giving.
Unless we can give and receive we can do neither.
All taking is a cul-de-sac.
It leads to unhappiness and unfulfilment.
If you hold onto the cupful it stagnates.
If you give your cupful to the ocean you have the ocean.
You choose either the limited or the whole.

Energy operates in a circuit as, for example, in electricity or as
    in farming: seed – harvest – compost – seed.
The spiritual world works in the same way.
The weeds we must keep out are the weeds of doubt.
When you give, have the experience of receiving an even greater
    gift.
If you feel real unity you are in fact giving to yourself.
When you give, do not have the experience of losing . . . or you
    will lose.
Manifestation follows our *inner* feelings.
Spiritual seeds return in multiplication.

If we let go of the idea that "these things are mine" it is easier
    to give.
Giving starts all processes.
Whatever we want – give it.
Our natural inclination in relationships is to hold on; whereas
    truly releasing someone (i.e. giving them away) they will
    always truly be with us.
But if we bind them we lose them to the exact extent that we
    bind them.

10

Let people go and they will find their right place – and so will
    you.
If you want to be free, set people free.
If you want to be prosperous, set your money free.
If you try to bind it and hold onto it, it stagnates and dries up.
By giving money with love we open the door to receiving.
If we want opportunities, give opportunities to others.
If we want to be loved, give love.
Giving love is free.
Don't do what some people do, which is to give love as an
    investment for the future in the hope of manipulating
    someone to do what they want.
The basis of all life is turning from being a taker to a giver.
Takers are people in the process of collecting supposed values in
    order to "be" someone.
Givers acknowledge that they are the whole – that they have it
    all already.
All they need to do is express it.

Takers and getters don't know who they are and stand little
chance of finding out.
Givers are on the road to discovery of the truth of Being.

Acknowledgement of others (seeing the God in a person) is a
    part of giving.
It touches their essence and calls forth the truth of their Being.
Acknowledgement (reminding a person of their Being) can have
    immediate results and that person may not bloom for
    several years.
Sowing the seed starts the process.
The seed we can give is the seed "I AM".
"I AM" is the source from which there is no separation.

When we become a giver we die to the past.
We seek only to express.
Thus we lose desires to acquire and desire only to express.
Expression is giving.

Gratitude is a part of giving – to take the attitude that
   everything is good – whether we perceive it as good or bad
   – and to be thankful.
Gratitude opens the heart.
If we observe our body and see what lowers or raises our energy
   we will find giving always raises our energy.
Gratitude also raises our energy.
Forgiving raises our energy.
Forgiving, in the sense of giving up an attitude about the need
to be right, raises our energy.
Forgiving leads to atonement (or at-one-ment) and is the
   process of returning everything to the one.
When you give, don't expect to receive from the person you
   gave to necessarily.
Give without strings.
Your return may come from a totally different source.
Giving is acknowledging a person's essence.
Your essence feels real contact with the essence of the person to
   whom you give.
Give without counting the cost (rather acknowledge the gain)
   and doors open to you.
When you give people their freedom they like being with you.
In their freedom they often *choose* to be with you.
Free beings will choose to be where there is love and space for
   them.

If an area of your life is stuck, you're either not giving or not
   giving up.

Examples of what you can give up:

resentment	hate
greed	doubt
being right	struggle
belief in duality	fear
jealousy	warfare
making people wrong	vanity

judgement	undue attachment
evaluation	disempowering people
reasons	being better than others
rigid opinions	(or less than others)
anger	formbound reality

Examples of what you can give:

money	cooking	cheering people up
things	acknowledgement	healing
connections	wisdom	teaching
artistic performance	time	forgiveness
making people feel that	support	vision
life is worthwhile	love	shelter
sowing seeds in others		
of spiritual aspects		

The go-getter is in an endless state of stress and need – often to the point of constipation.

The go-giver turns on the tap and creates room for even greater creativity to flow.

THE LAWS OF MANIFESTATION

The process of manifestation can be compared to the billiard
    ball technique.
First you "see" the billiard ball in the pocket.
Then you trust your instinct to dictate how to hit it.
You strike, and trust the balls to complete the manifestation of
    your image – the ball in the pocket.

Taking a photograph provides a more detailed analogy.
The five stages in manifestation are Vision, Clarification,
    Declaration, Preparation and Action.
Everything starts with a *Vision*, or what you "see".
There must be a context for action, or nothing will happen.
Select your subject.
Unless the vision is clarified and precise in its definition, the
    result will be fuzzy.
Clarification needs focusing.
Your vision remains at the idea level until you commit to
    doing it.
Declaration and commitment demand action.
You press the shutter.
With these three steps the photograph has been created.
The last two steps (*Preparation* and *Action*) are mechanical.
Preparation is not tampering with the film or camera and
    trusting the process.
Action is taking the film to be developed, the processing and
    collecting the prints.
We are certain to have the photographs.

If we trust the vision that we have, and clear the space for it
    within our consciousness and lives, and if we continue
    trusting it, it is bound to happen.

14

To put new furniture in a room, you need to clear out the old
    furniture.
If you want a new relationship, a new job or greater health, you
    must clear out all the old redundant thoughts, beliefs or
    relationships that clutter the mind.
A holiday couldn't manifest if you hadn't created a space for it
    in your diary.
We have to clear a time in which it can happen.
Act according to your intuition and inner direction.
Often the intuitive direction may seem illogical, but it has a
    surprising way of opening up an opportunity for your
    vision to manifest.
You may wish to manifest money, but the intuition you get is to
    give money.
The reasoning mind would consider that to be illogical and
    counterproductive.
Greater giving may be the one thing necessary to open the door
    to greater receiving.
Your problem was that you weren't giving enough.

The path is from the unformed to the formed.
We accept responsibility as co-creator.
Things happen in context, not by themselves.
We set frames within which all action can take place.
"I win, you win" creates a completely different relationship to
    "I win, you lose", and therefore brings a different result.

Many people in the world operate from the context of
    hopelessness.
"Starvation is inevitable" results in activities called "crisis
    relief" and "aid".
These support the view of hopelessness.
The new context is: "the end of starvation is possible by the end
    of the century".
This creates actions that are possible.
It creates the global will, sufficiency, and a strategy for ending
    hunger.

If we act from impossibility or inevitability, nothing can
    fundamentally change.

The tendency has been to study sickness to determine health.
This means living in the context "sickness".
Within this framework, the only thing possible is to discover
    "what is sickness".
To be healthy it is necessary to live in the context "health", and
    to study healthy people.
Eliminating sickness does not bring health.
We have been trained to look at what we don't want.
We then try to eliminate it with "We don't want sickness,
    disease, sin or unemployment".
This thinking pattern does not bring solutions.
Thinking of what we *do* want brings solutions.
It brings health, ease, aliveness, prosperity and employment.

By committing ourselves to something, we bring it into the *now*.
Commitment is a now experience and reminds us of our vision.
State all your goals as achieved in the here and now.
Seeing things as happening in the future holds them there, and
    so they can never manifest.
By having a vision of a future event as "now", you start the
    manifesting process.
Vision and heart (emotion) together lead to the appropriate
    action to bring results.
When the heart and mind are co-ordinated the power is
    unlimited.
Faith is a here and now power, not a belief.
Faith is seeing things happen here and now, despite what *seems*
    to be happening in the condition.
See *everything* in the now.
See the future as a now experience.
Create it the way you want it.
The best way to predict the future is to create it, and to have
    faith in your creation.

Create everything in your life as a *now* experience where it is
   already achieved.
Don't chase a future which will always run away from you.
Life is an infinite now experience.
It is not sequential as we tend to experience it when living in the
   context of "time".
We tend to think that we move inevitably from birth to death.
It would be equally true to say that we are moving from death
   to birth.
In the perspective of "oneness", there is only life.

The fundamental shift is from twoness to oneness, from our
   habitual body/mind duality to Being.
There is a time lag between the commitment and the
   manifestation.
In planting a seed, time elapses before the flower appears.
The planting of the seed ensures that the flower *will* come,
   providing the process is followed.
You don't plant a seed and then pick it up every five minutes to
   see how it is doing.
The things we fear will happen *do* happen, because they receive
   more energy.

The devil belongs to duality.
He cannot exist in oneness (Heaven).
Any belief in "devil" or in trying to defeat him is a fruitless
exercise, as it keeps you out of oneness.
The simplest way of practising is to be the *presence*.
If you are fully present, only Presence can exist.
The more we are present, the more we disappear, as there is no
   room for anything else.
Practising these principles is like mastering a sport or a musical
   instrument.
We have to keep working at it.

PROSPERITY

We often act as beggars begging for crumbs.
The truth is we are princes and princesses in our own kingdom
    if we would only realise it.
We have forgotten that we are prosperity itself.
It is our state of being.
The beggar mentality sees only with the senses of the physical
    body.
It sees us as this human form – made up of body, mind and
    emotions, struggling to find a place.
The beggar mentality sees life as "out there" and feels that we
    must somehow go out and get it.

When paying bills create "I always have enough money to pay
    my bills."
Give no space to the thought "I can't pay my bills".
Prosperity has nothing to do with a sum of money.
It is a state of being, a context within which we live.
We must turn within. The joy in front of us is to rediscover who
    we are and to come from the space of being.
Life becomes a discovery process or an "un-covery" process.
Through this process we discover the whole Self or "God Self".

We must align with Being beyond the mind constructed worlds.
In Being there is no time, so there is nothing we can *do* to
    become prosperous.
We are already there.
The task is to acknowledge and express it.

Our problem is that we often will not take responsibility for
    being prosperous and acknowledge our prosperity.
So we find ourselves in the beggar condition.

Once we take responsibility, we have the simple choice to live
    within a state of prosperity or a state of poverty.
This choice creates one of two contexts – the first an opening,
    "prosperity", the second a closing, "poverty".
The first an opportunity, the second a problem.

The usual way that people try to gain prosperity is to work at
    manipulating the condition.
That is manipulating and gathering togetner *things*.
The way I suggest is to look upwards . . . where there is open
    space.
Create there the vision of prosperity and then raise your
    condition to your vision.
A vision of prosperity will include health, love, happiness,
    fulfilment and supply.

In condition there is a lot of form – a lot that we have to
    manage – whereas in vision there is open space.
Instead of managing the limited conditions around us, learn to
    manage the space.
Forms "show up" within the space.
Instead of pushing (forcing) for the result, we are pulling for it
    from within.
Instead of managing people and things manage the space within
    which things happen.
Managing the space of prosperity means: hold the vision of
    prosperity for yourself and for the world, despite outward
    appearances (the condition).
Hold true to this and act according to intuition.
Take opportunities (new openings) as they present themselves.
Then prosperity tends to show up as if drawn by a magnet.
Be active – do not sit and wait for it to happen.
Faith (holding the vision) without works (appropriate action) is
    dead.
It produces no result.
Vision empowered with *emotion* plus *action* equals *result*.

We are not talking about the distinction between rich and poor.
Those are dual opposites, like god and devil, sickness and
    health, peace and war.
We are talking about thinking "prosperity" or thinking
    "poverty": two contexts in which we may or may not have
    money at any particular time.
The statement "I am prosperous but have no money at the
    moment" is consistent with the vision.
"I'm in poverty and I have money but it's never enough" is also
    true in the context "poverty".
A context of prosperity is a foundation of Being.
Apple trees are apple prosperous by their very nature.
Sometimes there are no apples on them.
No apples does not necessarily mean no prosperity.

All wealth is created in the mind first.
98% of the work is the creative inner work, while external
    action is only 2%.
Most people approach it the other way around with
    correspondingly less good results.
Prosperity is our state of Being.
All there is to do is to either express it or not.

See everything as good.
Even debts are helping us in our prosperity if we learn the
    lesson.
Debts can encourage us to open our prosperity and can teach us
    valuable lessons in the management of money.
It is prosperous thinking to pay bills in a spirit of gratitude.
Prosperity is here and now.
Create the feeling of prosperity within yourself.
Like learning to play the piano, we need to practise at being
    prosperous and doing what prosperous people do.
Working on our prosperity consciousness is a spiritual activity.

Money is an energy.
Give more out, and allow more in.

Express more, so that it circulates in your life.

If we cut the switch off, there is no flow.

If we don't have money we are probably not giving enough.

One of the major difficulties can be that we are not willing to give.

In this case receiving becomes taking, and taking is a cul-de-sac.

Takers dry up fast.

Giving and receiving are both a part of giving.

Become a good giver and a good receiver.

No-one is truly prosperous until everyone is.

Create a vision of prosperity for all.

Be definite with money if you want money to be definite with you.

State clearly what you want and go for it.

There is only one time to start and that's now.

Hold your vision and *get started.*

Don't wait until the circumstances are right – they may never be.

Start now and correct as you go.

A rocket is corrected many times in getting to the moon.

It did not start off in the one-time right direction.

It was the vision "rocket – moon" and the willingness to be corrected that got it there.

You don't have to know how to do every stage of it at the beginning.

Just start.

Fear of not knowing what to do stops people.

Prosperous people give money.

Give money, time, support, friendship, love; write, drive, cook, teach, paint, etc.

In so doing we open the door to receive.

Listen to your inner voice about how much you should give – something that really represents you.

Give with love, not with the experience of losing.

Know that your gift is generating wealth, and that it must
   return.
You give to yourself.
It is from lack of giving that we have poverty.
*For*give yourself for your fear of losing money.
As we experience ourselves, so we express to the world.
If I feel myself as worthless, then I'm obviously worth less, and
   thus not prosperous.

Use affirmations such as "I am a prosperous person and love to
   give and receive money", "The more I give, the more I
   receive", "I am a wellspring of divine supply", "I create
   wealth in myself and others".
Affirmations are useful to create the climate of thinking needed.
Stop *struggling* in the external 2%.
Realign with your inherent prosperity and go to work in the
   creative 98%.
The external 2% will follow *naturally*.
Rewards for successfully manifested vision and creativity are far
   higher than rewards for manual/mental work which can
   always be bought in the market place.

Be the programmer of your own computer mind.
Most of our "thinking" is only automatic reaction from our
   already programmed computer mind.
Real thinking is creating new thoughts . . . something that was
   not there before.
We create prosperity, love, friendship, joy and health out of
   thought.
That is *real* thinking.
In this state the past disappears from us and poverty is over.
You are your own paymaster.
No-one can give you anything until you give it to yourself.

HOW TO USE YOUR DREAMS

There is who we are and there are levels of dreaming.
Sleep dreaming and the so-called awake state are two examples
    of dreaming.
Both are examples of the reactive mind.
See dreams as mirrors of the mind reflecting the dramas created
    by us for us.
Dreams come in many types:
— mental spin (the discharge of a jumble of recent experiences
    – no sense),
— teaching dreams,
— foretelling the future/warning dreams that seem real,
— soul travelling dreams, etc.
These are examples of sleep dreams.
In the awake state the whole of our mind-created life is a dream
    – not to be seen as different from those of sleep.
Understand and use your dreams, they form a major part of
    who we are *not*!
By looking into their *un*reality, we understand who we are – our
    wholeness and our reality.
A dream is a reflection of consciousness, so that we can see
    ourselves more clearly.

Our self-created drama is there so we can learn.
We are the scriptwriter, director, *all* actors and the audience in
    the dream.
Realise it is totally our creation and don't make the mistake of
    thinking that the personalities in a dream are representing
    themselves.
They are merely images playing a role you have given them.
The premise is that there is only myself in the universe.
Everyone in my universe is put there by me.

My experience of everyone in the universe is my experience
   of *me*.
If I hate everybody, I hate myself.
If I criticise others, I criticise myself.
If I see poverty out there – it is my own poverty I see.
My world!

I created all the characters.
They all represent a part of me.
They are performing a dream that I have created so that I can
   understand *me* better.
This is true whether we are "awake" or asleep.
Observing and interpreting dreams is a spiritual activity – and
   an important part of our lives and discovery process.
The way to remember dreams is to be interested in remembering
   them.
If we are not interested and don't give them any value we are
   not likely to remember them.
We can use a technique for recording dreams such as keeping a
   pad or tape recorder by our beds.

Important things to record are key characters, the action and,
   above all, how you actually felt during the experience.
What were you actually experiencing while the drama was going
   on?
What you're experiencing determines what the dream is all
   about.
If while watching the drama I'm afraid, then the dream is about
   releasing a fear.
If I am angry or upset the dream is about releasing anger or
   upset.
If I experience love or other good feelings, the dream is
   encouraging me to open my heart.

Interpreting the action of a dream is a subjective thing.
The symbols we use are personal to us.

We can work out our *own* meanings from our experience of the dream.

Dream interpretation books can be misleading and confusing.

The purpose of all dreaming is to assist us to fully realise and express our lives.

Recurring dreams are unfinished business.

Don't get involved in the drama – look at the experience, and then *complete* it with consciousness.

A dream is about your universe.

If you have a disaster dream and the interpretation is that you *are* afraid your world is cracking up – heal the fear.

If you have a disaster dream about the future and you are *not* afraid, then the dream is an invitation for you to heal the situation so that it never happens.

This you do within yourself.

As the future is fluid you can heal the negative elements of the dream.

Otherwise why have the dream?

Use these examples of affirmations which start the healing process:

Fear of Poverty
"I am prosperous".
"As I give, I receive".
"The more I give, the more I receive".

Fear of Ill Health
"I am health".
"The source of my health is divine love".
"The more I participate in health, the healthier I am".

Fear of Criticism
"I blame no-one".
"No-one blames me".

Fear of Losing Love
"I am a loving person".
"I deserve to give and receive love".

Fear of Old Age
"I am immortal".

Fear of Death
"I am moving towards a new life".

Fear of Insufficiency
"I am naturally successful".
"Who I am is all I need".

Nothing is inevitable or inescapable.
If you get a preview of a possible future event such as a disaster
or a sickness for yourself or another you can work to release the
situation within yourself so that what would have happened
now doesn't.
Astrologers, psychics, fortune-tellers can read future events
given that there is no change in the mind condition.
However, if we bring consciousness to the mind condition, we
can change or dissolve such predictions.
The power of consciousness is senior to any prediction.

We can programme our mind to do almost anything: solve
problems, dream racehorse winners, new inventions, poems,
solutions to personal problems, etc.
It's a fabulous instrument – use it!
It is truly the genie of the magic lamp.
We programme our mind by giving it commands prior to going
to sleep.
"I wake up knowing which job to take".
"I wake up with a new idea for my business", etc.
The mind goes to work during sleep and produces the answer –
either as a dream, a hunch (intuition) or as knowing.
The mind will work wonderfully for you if you treat it with
respect.
Give it precise commands.

Start a dream book!

Writing your dreams down encourages your mind to work more actively to resolve the work you give it to do.

All dreams are good, even the so-called "nightmares".

They are just pointing to a fear you need to address.

Many so-called psychic and mystical experiences which claim to be authentic communications with higher realms or beings are nevertheless just dreaming.

They still fall within the definition of self-created experience.

Interpret your dream on the day you have it – as soon after having the dream as possible.

Otherwise you lose key elements of it.

Once we see our "awake" state as dreaming, too, we can see that we have a mind-creating universe.

I am the space that contains all form – in fact the whole universe.

My reality is what is permanent here and now.

Anything that is *not* permanent here and now is my dream.

Anything which is changing – has a beginning and end – is my dream.

Who I am is what is constant.

What changes is my dream.

All we do is bring forth our *being* in life.

All our job problems, relationship problems etc. are a dream that we have created in order to fully experience who we are.

By looking at it we get a bigger experience that we are the whole of it.

By mastering that, we master ourselves.

Everything becomes good.

(See also "Affirmations")

CELEBRATING THE SELF

It is time to celebrate the Self.
Fifty years ago all was male orientated and dominated --
    church, education, government, business and families.
The female aspect is beginning to return to the world.

Masculine aspects	Feminine aspects
– opposition/alternative	– complementary
– experts	– personal responsibility
– externalise	– internalise
– personal	– impersonal
– mind	– heart
– divide	– unite
– intellect	– intuition
– analysis	– synthesis
– domination	– cooperation
– pushing for results (promotion)	– pulling for results (traction)
– competitiveness	– participation
– reason	– awareness

These aspects are present in each of us...the left brain being the
    masculine and the right the feminine.
Mankind is opening the right brain once more after a long
    period of left brain activity.
Western man has been left brain orientated.
Eastern man has tended to be right brain orientated.
The balance is coming.
All shifts that are happening in the world at large are a direct
    result of the shifts that are happening in each of us.
Conflict is a masculine solution.

Russia and America are like two rams locked together in
conflict, the masculine solution is one knocking out the
other.
At bows and arrows level this game may be fine, but at a
nuclear level it is a disaster.
The feminine solution is cooperation or together finding a
solution.
Psychoanalysis is a male approach.
Problems are analysed to find solutions based on a belief that
the human psyche is a lot of bits to be placed in their right
compartments.
The female solution says that man is whole and calls him into
his wholeness.
The male aspects of promotion and the hard sell are now giving
way to traction – pulling individuals towards new ideas by
giving them a vision.

Experts, doctors, priests, professors, government know-alls
(exclusive experts "owning" their knowledge) are giving
way to individual responsibility – a balanced male-female
approach.
The female of "expertise" is "participation" a sharing rather
than an exclusive ownership of knowledge.
People are no longer impressed by experts – they would rather
listen to the people who *do* it.
Participate!

In business training methods and marketing the masculine
solution is: *pushing* for results often through the medium of
mechanical skills.
The feminine solution works more from vision and context with
intuition: *pulling* for results.
Naturally both male and female aspects are needed, but in
balance and working together.. As individuals we must now
bring the two hemispheres of our brain into cooperation.
From there we must reach out into the world with that same
spirit of cooperation.

Let go of a belief that conflict is the proper solution.
Don't let go of competition altogether, but have competition
     within co-operation.
A football match is a competition with winners and losers.
But all lies within the game "football", with which both sides
     are cooperating.
Democracy is true cooperation.
It is acknowledging we are all from the same source.
We are equal as beings, though we may have different positions
     in life, unequal possessions, etc.
We live within mutual respect for the source that we are.
We live in cooperation with one another as brothers and sisters
     in spirit.

Celebration is creating the context "celebration" and living
     within it.
"I now live life as a celebration."
"I celebrate life and am committed to seeing the good in life."
"I am creating life as a party to which all are invited."
There are good times and bad times, but I live within the
     framework of "celebration".
Awareness of heart and mind are essentials.
Survival is living in the condition of life as though it were all
     that there is.
Live life in a state of celebration rather than of survival.
Survival is hanging on.

Pain and suffering come because people will not let go.
People hold on to beliefs which limit them from expressing the
     truth.
We can let go and release these.
We reject ourselves and feel that we are rejected.
Why do we reject ourselves?
Do we feel unworthy, unlovable?
Is there some statement about ourselves which is holding us
     from other people?
All of these beliefs are untrue at the level of Reality.

They all deny the truth that we *are* love.
We create false armoury, then live in it as if it were true.
This results in a sense of hurt.
Pain means we are not trusting.
We put our attention on believing things which are less than
    who we really are.
Stop looking at the "evidence" of the world – look in the Self.
Adventure is turning vision into a physical reality.
We always have enough for what we want.
We celebrate money by giving it.

Give up all of the things we no longer need – things,
    relationships, attitudes, beliefs.
The ultimate reality is I AM.
Give up death!
If we believe it to be a reality we live in preparation for death.
Reverse this to "Life is a preparation for life" (at worst) or
    "Life *is* life" (at best).
Create the new context "There is only life".
Then the belief "I am born and I die" loses its meaning.
It no longer has the significance of a beginning and ending.
Create the context "There is only one".
Explore this new reality.
Before we saw "many human beings."
Now we see one "human beingness" with many examples.

Create the contexts: "Celebration", "Love", "Oneness",
    "Relationship", and "A world for you and me".
Put your attention on the context and act out of intuition.
Create "There is only health".
In this new context sickness becomes a part of health.
It is no longer an opposition to health to be knocked out by
    some drug.
It becomes an opportunity to recognise the dis-ease that we are
    experiencing.
Thus we can realign with our health.
Listen to your intuition and it leads you back to health.

If you create the context "Life is miserable" all you get is a spin
of your bad luck tapes.
Hell is having no vision.
Have a vision of celebration and misery is transformed.
Hell becomes heaven.

Life is healing.
Our joy is to return the whole to the whole.
I return myself to the whole.
I *am* the whole.
Healing thus returns one to one.
In the context "Oneness" the thought "You over there and me
over here" is no longer sustainable – there can now only
be Here.
It follows that in order to heal you over there I must heal me
over here (a fundamental principle of healing).
All condition is spiritual condition.
Healing someone "over there" can only be partially useful.
Real healing only arrives when it is changed from the inside.
You may be caught up in a belief that you are ill, which you
must release.
I see you as healthy.

The context of "Giving" opens us.
"Receiving" is an indispensable part.
"Sharing" contains both.
If we need things to make us happy, we also believe that in their
absence we must be miserable.
Yet our happiest moments are never associated with things, but
with the experience of being in the "Now" (i.e., when we
are being creative).
Happiness is being creative in the present.
Happiness is accepting the way it is at this moment, and in
creating the future we want now.

Transform all your yesterdays!

Do not live in the fear that things you did were wrong or that
   you took a wrong direction.
Create that all your yesterdays were exactly right in bringing
   you to your now.
"I love you" means I recognise that you are God expressing.
To love another person is to see God.
To *see* another person is to see God.
See with the single eye.
Looking at ourselves, all we can see is an "Am-ness".
If we see any "twoness" then we have come into our mind, a
   strata of energy that operates in a dualistic way with
   positive-negative.
Only when that comes to rest – neutrality – is oneness achieved.

Celebrate your body!
Look inside – you don't feel age.
The only signs of age are external.
Growing old is only an idea.
Practise birthdays going backwards, "unbirthdays", and your
   body will go back with your concept.
The law of psychosomatics: the body follows the instructions of
   the mind.
The truth is that everything is fine.
We are all perfect, but we have hypnotised ourselves that we are
   not.
Remove the bits of false self-hypnosis to discover that all is
   O.K.

Celebrate someone you know well and don't like.
For example, this new viewpoint could read:
"Everything about that individual is good."
"They never did anything wrong."
"Their contribution was to force me to discover who I am, learn
   how to love, learn what space for others is and learn what
   freedom, strength and courage are."
"I see them as good and let go of my belief that they are evil."
"In releasing them I release myself and I become liberated."

"To be free I must let go of everyone else (they will often come closer to me as a result)".

Create a life of celebration and share it with others.

HOW TO DISSOLVE ATTITUDES

An attitude is a position in the mind – a belief that we hold
  onto.
When we take a position we create right and wrong.
We tend to see attitudes as "my" attitude rather than as "an"
  attitude.
When we see it as "an" attitude, we can be more willing to
  release it.
We see that it has no value, or is limiting the quality of our life.
Identify our negative attitudes and see the prison we have
  created for ourselves.
To identify, look at the condition of life that we're in.
Pin down our hidden statement.
Mind is a computer – a multi-level device.
It is programmed out of what we experience, and dependent on
  our context.
90% of all life determining mental statements are logged by the
  age of 9.

No event happens by chance.
We create all that happens to us.
Create the attitude that everybody is on our side, even when it
  doesn't look that way.
You will find that they will become a contribution to your life.
You can be grateful to them, and dissolve your attitudes.
Change a statement like "People I love reject me" to "I am
  love, and so is everybody else".
Stay with that, and other limiting statements will come up for
  you to release by changing the thought and "being with"
  the feeling until it releases.
One way to dissolve unwelcome statements is to turn them into
  jokes.

35

"Resent" means to re-feel.
You keep experiencing the same negative emotion.
You create the feeling again.
If you resent, there is definitely something to dissolve.

We must become aware that we are not the mind, but rather the
   space that contains the mind.
We are the space that contains attitudes, which we can attach to
   or release at will.
Releasing attitudes does not in any way damage who we are.
It creates space to see things from a different perspective.
Personality (our mask) is the sum total of our attitudes.
We can see our persona as a thought construction.
It is a scaffolding that we have created, based on our own
   experiences plus the prevailing attitudes of our parents,
   church, social grouping, etc.
This construction is *not* us as Being.
The fundamental attitude that limits us and the cornerstone of
   all attitudes is the belief that we are beings *separate* from
   the source.

The way to release attitudes is to:
— Acknowledge who we are – a formless expression of love.
— Trust.
— Look honestly at the attitude, see whether it is useful (which
   it usually isn't) and release it.
— Let love fill the space.

When we release a fundamental attitude a whole series often
   collapses much like a chain of falling dominoes.
Undo attitudes rather than adopt positive thinking, which tends
   only to be cosmetic.
Positive thinking as a mental process creates negative thinking
   by giving form to its opposite.

Create an I AM book.
Catch your limiting attitudes.

Turn them round into life-supporting statements.

Then write them in the book for reinforcement.

This becomes a wonderful tool for transforming the quality of our life.

"If only I had what he has" becomes "I am grateful that X shows me the potential that I have".

"I am jealous of Y" becomes "I am grateful to Y for showing me the relationship that is possible to me".

"I am rejected" becomes "I am included".

"I don't have enough money" becomes "I am a prosperous being".

"No-one loves me" becomes "I am a loving being and everyone loves me".

We use only a small portion of our full potential.

By working consciously on ourselves we can increase the amount of our potential used.

Self love is loving the divine Self as us.

Love is not a person – it is a state of Being expressed through feeling.

Parents frequently run our lives even when they are not physically present.

They exist in our consciousness, they live in our thinking.

Wherever we are their voice speaks in us.

They can even run our lives from beyond the grave, ie: a domineering parent can run our life until they are released in consciousness from having that control.

The beginning of freedom from domination is recognising that we are being dominated, manipulated or controlled.

This also raises the question, are we sub-consciously doing it to them (see Mirror Principle)?

How does looking from a different viewpoint help me to cope?

I see it as it is (a loving parent), rather than the way it is misinterpreted by my senses and conditioning (a nagging parent).

Releasing a position gives us an opportunity to see intuitively the unreality of that prevailing viewpoint.

We see things inx a more enlightened way.
What is the difference between reason and intuition?
With reason we have our solutions on past evidence.
Reason is always looking into history (the mind).
With intuition we are in the now, uncluttered by any mental
concepts (such as past thinking).
Without a commitment to purpose nothing really changes.
Purpose is a statement of our commitment in the now.
When committed, our unconsciousness (traumas, unfinished
business, etc.) of the past will come up for dissolution.
Then those attitudes which are stopping us from fully living can
be released.

What is the psychology of personal repair?
It is raising ourselves in a state of consciousness through the
prevailing attitudes of:

<pre>
                wrong
         wrong   wrong
         right   wrong
         wrong   right
         right   right
                right
</pre>

"wrong" is the very lowest level, total non-participation in life
with no communication.
"wrong wrong" is limited participation but total opposition
(permanent upset).
"right wrong" is the attachment to my attitudes being the right
ones, thus yours are the wrong ones (leads to argument
and upset).
"wrong right" is "right wrong" reversed.
"right right" is the position in which I believe my attitudes are
right and acknowledge that your attitudes are right (this
leads to discussion).
"right" is acknowledging there is only one source and *everything*
is Right – so you see everything as a contribution.

This calls for wholeness.

This series is a practical tool for seeing how you are doing, and how to assist others up the scale.

All energy is a circuit.

By speaking love, money, health, we start the circuit.

We are our speaking and if we keep our word our speaking is Truth.

What is forgiveness?

Forgiveness is giving up your attitudes.

It is releasing the belief that anything is wrong.

Thus the condition returns to the source.

It is not the good me forgives the bad you, which is still an attitude and releases nothing.

Nature is a whole and pulls for wholeness.

All "God" expression pulls for wholeness.

It is its nature.

People who express themselves get younger every day.

They progress towards birth.

Dissolving attitudes makes me younger.

N.B. The psychology of personal repair was first made known to the author by Chuck Spezzano, Ph.D.

TAKING RESPONSIBILITY

There was an Irishman who was very proud of his village.
He considered it to be a very special village
When asked why this village was so special he answered
    "My village is special because from here I can get to
    anywhere I want to in the world."
The point of the story is that from *here* we can get to anywhere.

If we start from a false position we get nowhere.

Making deep inquiry into ourselves is the greatest work we can
    do. When we find a new level of our own selves, it is a
    great advance. This is the age of consciousness.
The age of intellect is passing.
Intellect is making way for "being" as the major focus.
The old way was to use the mind to dominate.
There was always a need to have power over others.
"I must dominate in order to be someone".
This does not lead to mastery.
The new way is to generate power and to empower others to be
    themselves.

Transformation begins when we take responsibility.
Taking responsibility does not mean taking the blame.
It means acknowledging that I am the source of what's so.
The old way of seeing the future was based on looking into the
    past and projecting a future.
This is a reasoned future.
The better way is to look from vision and create the future we
    want.

There is no such thing as a predictable definite future that
cannot be changed by taking responsibility, looking in
vision, and creating a new future.

We tend to look in the mind for "THE answer".
The mind does not have "THE answer".
It is a mechanism.
It can only give answers according to its programming.
The aware perception *is* : "I AM THE answer".
Many people are waiting for the guru – "Baba" – to take them
there.
We must take responsibility for being here and see any guru as
a mirror.
He only reminds us of what we already Know.

Every cell has total knowing.
Each cell is perfect in itself.
Matter cannot be sick.
Sickness in the body is merely suppression of the Truth.
Sickness is attachment to damaging mind programmes.
In awareness we can listen to the cells.

Just as we have a physical body we have a universal body.
We can train ourselves to see the world within us.
With this perspective we cease to feel separated.
By surrendering our attachment to the physical body we find
ourselves in the universal body.
Encourage each cell to be responsible – which it is only too
happy to do, given the opportunity.
Compare the human body and the universal body.
Every cell in the human body being totally responsible leads to
every human being in the universal body being totally
responsible.
This is the vision of the transformed world and would lead
mankind to his next level.
When we dwell in the universal body we recognise that the
Essence, the core, the very basis of all of us is the same.

41

If you're the universe what can be outside you?

When we dwell in oneness we are the looker, the looked at and
the looking – all three as one.
We let go of the "thisness" of me.
A fundamental climate of thinking that persisted in the world
until recently was a "you or me" (conflict).
The current climate of thinking which is emerging is "you and
me" (partnership).
The step yet to be taken is "you are me" (union).

All people want to love and be loved.
This is the very essence of us.
Thus who are we? Love! There is only love.
A community ("coming into unity") is a group which
acknowledges the oneness of creation.
It is not the membership of a club.
Since there is only love, all that we perceive differently is what
we need to transform.
If there is only love, I have everything here and now, even if I
don't see it.
Healing is returning everything to love.
Healing is dissolving the beliefs created by the intellect and
carried out by the emotions.

The mind world is full of belief systems – medical, political,
religious, social, etc.
These are systems of thinking.
They are not creative and loving in themselves.
If there is only love what is disease?
It's a loving reminder to realign with being.
Treat it with gratitude.
Listen to what it is saying and take the appropriate actions.

Use vision.
Vision is seeing, not imagining.
Imagining is creating fantasies.

Vision is an act of creation.

Backed with commitment and faith it will produce the physical state of the vision.

We can declare a vision with the spoken word.

Speaking words has power if we learn to mean what we say and if we are someone who keeps our word.

To take an idea and make it happen is the training ground for life.

Vision is an act in consciousness.

That which you can see you can manifest.

Live in your vision.

Any organisation, business or person loses itself if it loses its vision.

Hold on to your vision against all negative views and conditions.

If you hold it, your vision pulls your thinking in the direction of your vision.

Life is an expansion into Itself.

Traumas help you find deeper levels of yourself.

I am responsible – but where does my responsibility end?

If I dwell in the universal body, my responsibility is to the whole universe and all that it contains.

In taking responsibility we must let go of our beliefs in a limited being.

Allow ourselves to acknowledge.

Expand into divine being where only oneness exists.

Thus all is God and all is good.

By surrendering to the "God-ness" that is the I AM, the "mind-ness" that I am is transcended and transformed.

The job that we have is to transform the physical plane of consciousness – to spiritualise it and liberate it.

The idea of ducking our responsibility, sitting on a mountain and reaching Nirvana, is at best only half the job and at worst a cul-de-sac.

By living in our vision and acting in our commitment we grind
up the conditions that persist.
We transform them and raise them to our vision.
Power comes in mastering form.
What you are passionately interested in, is the will of God.
When we take responsibility we radiate outwards from a
constant fullness.

HOW TO FIND A VOCATION

When you are clear on your purpose, when you know what you
    are here to do, your vocation will become obvious.
No-one can give you a purpose.
It is a decision you must take.
It is the answer to the question "What do I really want to do
    with my life?".

If you see life as a house or a mansion of consciousness you
    must be clear on who is living there.
Is it a home for a healer, an entertainer, someone committed to
    sufficiency, prosperity, nutrition, loving relationships?
Who is living there?
When you know who is to live in the house then you can make
    the proper design.
Most people try to find their purpose by looking into the
    condition of their life.
It is not found there.
It is found in vision.

To discover purpose go into contemplation until you reach the
    Alpha state (about 7 – 13 Hz).
Use any technique you like to get you there, stilling, countdown,
    etc.
In the Alpha state the right brain functions more.
The left brain is the mechanical brain.
It works more in Beta (between 13 and 30+ Hz.).
Most people try to find solutions to problems in the awake
    state.
They are not to be found in that part of the mind.
They need the activity of the right brain in the Alpha state.
At the Alpha level you *know* what you want to do.

The key to purpose is service.
Once you serve others you find that you are served.
Working genuinely for other people, you benefit.
For a vocation to be satisfying it must be of service.
It is not what you *do* that matters but who *you* are that's
    doing it.

Most people look for a job rather than create the vocation that
    they want.
Ideally they do it themselves or make the vocation that they've
    created available to an employer.
Often people find looking for employment to be boring or
    depressing.
They have no enthusiasm for it.
The basic reason for this is "being employed" is not creative.
It does not in any way fulfil individual purpose.
We either consciously or unconsciously are aware of this.
Hence the feelings of hopelessness and depression in job
    hunting.

When we create in vision the vocation we really want, based on
    service and purpose, and then set about finding a way of
    doing it, our enthusiasm returns.
"I am looking for a job in finance" is boring.
"My vision is that everyone should be financially potent and
    I am committed to playing my part to bringing this about"
    is exciting.
"I am looking for a job as a gardener" is very small thinking.
"I want to spend my life gardening human beings, animals and
    plants so that they blossom into their full beauty" is a
    wonderful vision.
"I am looking for a job in personnel" is uncreative.
"I am committed to fully supporting people in creating the lives
    they want" is a creative vision.

Ask yourself "How do I want to love my fellow man on this
    planet?"

The truth is that everybody wants to contribute to mankind's
    wellbeing.
But few have allowed and stirred themselves to think about it.
Look along your purpose line and ask yourself "Whom do I
    wish to serve and how do I wish to serve them?"
If my purpose is to entertain – whom do I wish to entertain?
How do I wish to entertain them?
This will lead you to your occupation.
A useful exercise is to write down ten things that you really love
    doing.
At least two or three of these should be part, and ideally more,
    of your life work.
If what you are doing for a living does not appear in your list
    of things you love to do, you're in the wrong job.
Look anew.
Any moment spent in an activity you don't love is a waste of
    time and uncreative.
You are suppressing life with such an activity.

The present boom industry is human resources – raising people
    in their state of consciousness.
In your vision, life is exciting.
In your vision a vocation emerges of which you never get tired.
Our vision is our gift of love to the planet.
The business of job selection can be reversed so that the
    applicants, examining the job, see whether it fits them.
With this system they select themselves.
This avoids all sorts of hidden undercurrents.
The applicants really speak the truth to themselves.

Once found, hold the vision.
Commit to it and you'll find all your past experience is useful
Don't throw your experience away.
If your training is as an accountant, you'll find these skills and
    knowledge will naturally be a part of your vision, or at
    very least, part of the experience that you gained.
Nothing is wasted.

WHY SUFFER?

Only you can change your life.
Many expect others to make their life work for them.
The solution to either physical or emotional problems is not
    outside us.
Don't belong to the "I'm right" club with a membership of one.
Straightening other people out never works.

Physical pain is a warning, essential for the preservation of our
    body.
Mental pain is only a condition which is unnecessary.
Some religions require suffering.
Suffering is mental and emotional attachment.
There is another way of looking at it.
If we *are* suffering, look at the "why" and then let it go.
The key is to be able to live in this moment.
Take the suffering – upset, jealousy, unloved, unwanted and
    question:
"What is it really that is suffering?".
"Am I suffering?".
"Is it I who is jealous, or am I experiencing jealousy?".
This means rediscovering who we are, and who we are not.

Man has been trained to align his mind with the condition of
    life.
This results in: "What I see in the condition is true".
Our training says that what the senses tell us is reality.
We are a body/mind complex.
Our senses do not tell us of our greater depth.
Our senses see no money in the bank and tell us we are poor.
With this method of seeing we feel separation, and can never
    find that "something" to make us whole.

Behind our mask or persona we risk having considerable fear.

We fear getting old, getting sick, failing, how a thing is going to turn out.

Such fears go on inside many people.

Our image is a lie which we keep up for fear of losing the affections of our friends.

In trust, or in love, we can drop this facade – of the conditions which we find in the mind.

Mind is like a radio signal – a band of consciousness which we walk into at birth.

It includes the previous thoughts in our field, plus the conditioning of our religion.

We find ourselves in this forest, just as we find ourselves in our national and social groups.

We live in their conditions.

Educational and family structures are also imposed on us.

If we align to these conditions, that is all we have.

Fighting a fog does not overcome it.

We need to dissolve it, or else rise up and find a higher place.

Someone needs to dissolve the fog, for there to be any real transformation.

This set of thoughts, dwelling in a mass of thoughts, brings us mental pain.

Dwelling in the stillness of being, which knows only the present, is the way out.

We live in all of this past thinking, instead of living in the present.

You cannot unite people who live in this condition of mental fog, even if you group them together, or even tie them together.

The mental structure is *separation*, so there is no unity in the structure of the mind.

It only sees "I'm right, you're wrong".

To unite the world we must go a different way.

We must discover that we are one already and uniting is
    unnecessary.
To do this we must go inwards and explore ourselves, and our
    different states of being.
Only thus can we hope to change our external conditions.
If we look within, we begin to see who we are *not*.
We can see that the conditions which bind us are a mental and
    emotional mass which exists apart from us.
We can let them go.

If I feel anger in a relationship, using my "separationist" mental
    approach, my inclination is to hold onto the relationship,
    to try to bind that person to me.
Should that person do something other than my mental and
    emotional addictions want, I am in pain.
If I have anger against my mother, be aware that she's fine.
It's just that I hold onto a mass of thoughts and emotions about
    her which create a barrier.

It is essential to realise who is running my life.
Is it mental attitudes implanted by my mother and father, my
    church, my social group, my national thinking or political
    bias?
Are these running my life or am I?
If I'm to be free, I must stand at the centre of my being.
I must unplug all the thoughts or emotions that control me.
This is done in consciousness, in meditation, in the inner silence.
Many people's actions are merely rebelling against the mental
    structures they find themselves in.
Don't rebel against the mental structures, which only intensifies
    them.
Stand rather at the centre of being.
Dissolve the attitudes and create anew.

We must release (forgive) father, mother, teacher, preacher, so
    that their imaginations don't run our life.

Sometimes our ideal image of Prince or Princess Charming pulls
　　us constantly into the future.
This image is a barrier to us.
It stops us enjoying the life and people that are present now.
With ideals such as these, we reject all of those who don't live
　　up to that image.
We are in danger of missing life entirely.

Many ideals and attitudes pull us into the future.
We often find that we are doing what we "ought" to do or
　　"should" do rather than what we want to do.
Dissolve the oughts and shoulds which only bring slavery.
They are not the mark of the free man and woman.
Healing our universe creates space.
We do this by forgiving and surrendering all conditioning that
　　binds us to the past and future.

Begin to feel the "presence" in you.
You might then realise that the presence *is you*.
Align mind with being.
It is like looking upward at the sun instead of the muddy water
　　of condition.
Look up!
If we look at beautiful, loving relationships, that's what we find.

If we criticise and look for faults, that's what we find.
Give out generous thoughts and you will receive them back.
Don't agree with criticism and thus add to it.

In a relationship about which you have emotional pain, look at
　　what you are holding on to.
What are you unwilling to let go?
Usually it is a thought that the other person is wrong.
Is that true, or just what I'm thinking?
Who decides: society, me, religion?
Are they *really* wrong, or have I just joined with those
　　thoughts?

51

They never loved me!
Is that true, or just my point of view?
By changing the viewpoint to a compassionate one, the whole
   picture changes.

My making others wrong does not help them.
Perhaps they are already looking at the muddy water.
Help them to see the sun!
This creates a mutual healing and reestablishes friendship.
This is living in the now – not in the fears from childhood days.
Unshackle the past and the future.
Release all the conditions which we think bind us.

Beware of looking with the senses.
They tend to look at conditioning.
Do we look *at* a window and see the fly on it?
Do we look *through* the window and see the garden beyond?
Do we allow our attitudes to stand in the way of the divine
   being that is beyond?
With this sensual model we look out of our little selves and see
   only our limitations.
We speak not the truth, but according to the conditions of our
   thinking.

Structures in themselves aren't bad or wrong.
The mind can only work with structures.
Check that the structures you are using are useful.
To live in the structure "people reject me" is not useful.
"I include myself in life" is a more useful structure.
"I don't have enough" is not a useful structure.
"I always have enough" is more useful.
All statements are equally true.
It depends on the value that we give them.
Give value to the statements and climates of thinking that are
   useful.
Present opportunities rather than problems.

Discussing problems with another person in a negative way only adds to the problem.

Getting involved in other people's beliefs about their sickness only adds to their sickness.

The truth of being that WE ARE stands free of negatives and sickness.

One law of psychosomatics is that the body follows exactly the instructions of the mind (as expressed in thoughts and emotions).

If our body is sick, we can be certain that in some way we have instructed it to be that way.

Knowing this we can reverse it and bring about healing.

Another law is that the mind is limited by the habitual emotional attitudes locked in the body's muscular behaviour.

Pain is a resistance to being.

Physical pain is useful.

It acts as a warning and stops us overusing damaged parts.

This is not the case with emotional pain.

Pain is thus a resistance to life.

"I'd rather have my 'poor me' story than express life".

Our "poor me" story is often developed in childhood with resultant tantrums, sickness and disasters, because we found that brought us attention.

Since what we really want is to love – attention is not sufficient.

We should grow up, be adults and release ourselves from our childish thinking and feeling.

We find the causes of our attachments at the Alpha level where we can release them.

Otherwise we repeat our addictions and behave in mind loops.

Psychologically painful conditions lead to physically painful conditions later.

An accident is often the result of intensely held psychological pain or a belief in accidents.

Most pain can be healed with forgiveness.

Forgive means give up your attitudes and beliefs.
Most things can be healed at Alpha.
Fifteen minutes a day as a regular practice for everyone.
Two times fifteen minutes for chronic cases.
Three times fifteen minutes per day for life-threatening ones.
Maybe ten percent of all conditions need work at Theta.
Meditation work at Alpha and Theta strengthens the immune
    system.
In meditation problems appear and disappear in the space.
In oneness there is no room for duality.

Think of the flow of life as a river.
Let go and flow with it.
Being still inside is the road to happiness.
It regains our own individual sovereignty.
There's no peace of mind – rather peace from mind.
Peace is a quality of being.
Explore the still waters of our inner being.
This is a practical approach to the ending of suffering both for
    ourselves and for others.

GENIUS

We think that there are only a few geniuses (most of whom are
dead).
The truth is that at some level of our being we are all geniuses.
It is merely a question of releasing our genius . . . a more
expanded state of consciousness.
We all have the following levels of consciousness, identified by
the speed of the brain waves:
Beta level – eyes open, awake state: the outer, objective world,
13-30Hz.
Alpha – half way between awake and asleep (meditation level):
inner world, 7-13 Hz.
Theta – mind and pain disappear: key to painless childbirth,
4-7 Hz
Delta – unconsciousness – deep sleep but in fact state of high
awareness, 1/2-4 Hz.

Sleep is a cycle through Alpha, Theta and Delta.
Most of the awake state is spent with Beta predominant, which
represents only 1% of our capability.
Only geniuses have been fully aware of these other states, and
have found how to use them simultaneously.
Mind is necessary in the outer world, roughly divided into Beta/
mechanical, Alpha/creative.
Unless we are aware, we operate as conditioned beings – totally
mechanical.
But who is the conditioner?
We are.

The way into earthly life is through Delta – and it is also the
way out.
A profound mystical experience is a "conscious" Delta state.

Most people alternate between a predominance of Beta activity
and sleep, not consciously using the creative aspects of
Alpha and Theta.
Our genius operates mostly at Alpha.

Imagine an ideal house with your eyes closed.
It is completely describable.
That is your genius at work.
That which you can see and imagine you can produce in the
physical world.
Where the eye is single (imagination) there is only one.
In general terms the left brain looks into history to decide who
I am.
The right brain sees the whole and lives in the now.
The left brain is the reactive, logical mind.
Genius is self-bestowed – if we take personal responsibility for
awakening it.

At the genius level we know things that we've never learnt or
been told.
Many geniuses were simple and uneducated people.
They just had this other knowing.
However it's not exclusive to them.
We can work for it in our Alpha, Theta and Delta states.
A way to awaken genius is to desire something greatly.
To desire something greatly to serve humanity is even more
potent.
If the desire is just for me, I'm limited to my personal energy.
If the desire is for mankind, my energy is unlimited.
We find ways which are entirely new.
We gain our sovereignty.

There's nothing you can think of which is impossible.
Cultivate thinking the impossible.
Keep asking the question "What if?"
What if the outside is inside?
What if the outside world and the inside are the same place?

What if man can fly?
What if it were possible to be in two places at the same time?
What if we don't need telephones to talk to each other at a
    distance?

In meditation open to new ideas.
Let them float into our minds like "God-children", nurture
    them, help them grow, until the ideas begin to flower.
It's like planting seeds.
The seed is the idea.
Consciousness is what it needs to help it grow.
The idea is yours – work with it.
Don't give it away until it is ready.
Then only take it to the right place – a place it can be used.
It would be hard selling freezers to the Eskimos.

We can programme our minds to answer problems.
The answer usually comes as a metaphor.
As you go to sleep give instructions to the mind that you will
    awaken with the solution.
Or drink half a glass of water and programme that, on drinking
    the other half, the answer will come.
Study nature.
All the great ideas and inventions come from nature.
Be playful.
Often ideas develop when we're being childlike and having fun.
If we keep asking questions, ideas come up.

Using genius is not only for use in the creation of inventions or
    the arts, but in every moment.
In every moment we can use our genius to create.
Create "there's only love", "there's only health", or "prosperity
    for all".
We can use our genius to BE cause.
The greatest genius is to live every moment as cause.
Be at cause and create a nourishing, exciting and loving world.

The law of mind is "what you put your attention on increases".
Put your attention on creative, loving and prosperous ideas and they increase accordingly.
Make sure you have a notebook to capture these ideas and develop them.
You, too, can be a genius.

RELATIONSHIPS I

There is only one relationship.
That is a relationship with your Self (the Divinity).
That Self lives as all people.
Thus I see my reflection in you and see only Divinity.
The viewpoint of duality, "you" and "me" being separate,
    misses the essence of relationship.
In duality we see two separate people seemingly separate in their
    thinking and behaviour.
We see twoness.
Most therapies try to solve problems from a twoness
    perspective.
All struggle comes from seeing from the dualistic point of view.

The enlightened way is to acknowledge *one* supreme source,
    thus one relationship.
As the one source is love, there *is* only love.
If I see you as love (you may have forgotten that you are)
    I remind myself that I am love.
The essence of relationship is thus present.
The more I can dissolve my barriers to the truth of my Being,
    the more I can be with you.
Rather than trying to sort another person out, work to dissolve
    your own barriers with that person.
Trying to sort them out comes from the belief that they are
    wrong and you are right.
This limiting attitude is not based in truth.

Remember who we are (a formless expression of love) and that
    we are already in relationship.
It is also true that we express as form or concentrated energy.

Placing our attention on the form severely limits us and gives us the sense of separation.

When we acknowledge our Selves as Being and free from limiting forms, mind statements that we attach to such as "I can't relate", "No-one loves me", "I'm rejected", "I'm not good enough", and "It's hopeless" can be seen as the cheats that they are.

They limit our experience of being Love.

We can release these mind statements and exclude them from our being.

This greatly raises the quality of our life and relationships.

With a viewpoint of oneness we are already in love.

As love, any barriers between us can be dissolved and our differences enjoyed.

The way is naturally found.

As there is only love, hate and anger must also be aspects of love.

You must love someone very much to hate them, or why bother with all that energy.

When we address within ourselves our resistances to love, we will find these aberrations of love will disappear.

The hand that seems to strike us becomes a hand of love.

Love is here and now.

Thus it is wherever *here* and *now* exist.

In love I can expand to my Universal Body containing all things.

I can release those whom I love and not try to hold on to them.

Since I am them and they are me, the aching for physical proximity disappears.

It is of course fine for people to be together if it is appropriate.

My interest is far more that they are free to express their lives in a way that is right for *them*, rather than that they should fit a pattern that *I* have prescribed for them.

Love is a present experience.

Either you are experiencing it or you are not.
Trying to recapture love from the past, that has no present
    reality, is like trying to re-eat old meals.

Relationship is an opportunity to work out our incompletion.
We rediscover our wholeness.
It is a lesson in learning how to love.
The experience of love is independent of sex, though the
    expression of sex correctly used is an expression of love.
Sometimes a gay relationship is an incompletion being worked
    out.
A commitment to a relationship will bring up the barriers to it.
When you commit to it, you soon find out what you have to
    do.
In the context "I am afraid of marriage", if I'm committed I
    will work on myself and dissolve that fear.
If I'm not committed, the fear will stand in the way of
    discovering the true relationship.
Thus the key to relationships is commitment.
Making a commitment leads you to the truth of the
    relationship.

Mind statements are barriers to relating.
We can either let the mind statements win, such as "I'm not
    good enough", "No-one loves me" etc, or we can take
    responsibility for dissolving them, and having satisfying
    relationships.
If you find yourself unable to relate to certain people, then it is
    most probably something in your *own* consciousness that
    you need to resolve.
When you really are your Self, you relate to everyone.
You are attracted to people in whom you see yourself more
    fully.
Your ideal life partner is the part of your Self that you seek
Ultimately you will only find it within your Self.

Personal love is a belief in twoness and is fear based unless
    expressed within unconditional love.
"Unless you love me, stay with me, let me own, possess and
    manipulate you, you don't love me".
"If you start doing something I don't want, I get upset".
Most people live their lives like that.
That is not a love relationship, but entanglement and
    manipulation.
They are trying to dominate each other.
"You must fit *my* box as a personality".
Personal love is much less than unconditional love, which says I
    love you anyway, so you're free to do as you choose.
The bottom line for all people is "I love you".
Once you feel it, you treat each other with respect.
You are no longer in pain and misery when others don't do
    what you want.

The mind functions with desire and fear.
We desire someone, do everything to conquer them, then fear
    we will lose them.
That is a poor relationship in comparison with being free, and
    sharing love, which is bigger than both.
Conditional love operates from our senses and fears.
It pushes away.
Pure, unconditional love draws.
If you can heal one relationship, you can heal them all, because
    you have the formula.

Love is not a person – it's a space.
The basis of love is to know that you are *whole and complete*.
Therefore you share yourself, but are not dependent on each
    other emotionally.
The picture is of two wholes coming together – not two halves.
It is paranoia to think that we are missing one half.
We are not a vacuum cleaner sucking in love nor do we throw a
    psychic net around our victim, so he or she can't escape.
Love to another means freedom for them.

Grieving helps no-one – it only avoids living life.
Live fully.

All relationships are learning how to love.
Not I need you, want you, must control you – this is lust.
Relationships are dynamic.
A block with someone else can be overcome by sharing the
barrier.
All relationships are *with yourself*.
The barriers are the bits in you which aren't working, which
indicate an incompletion you need to heal in yourself.
You always choose the right partner.
There is no such thing as a negative response, when you hear
with ears of love.
All communication is an attempt to give and receive love.
If it's anger, the person is in pain with themselves.
Capture their upset: "If you feel like telling me, I'm here".
Share an experience, but not an opinion.
"I feel upset", not "You did something wrong – you don't love
me – it's all your fault".
Don't make others wrong.
You are, in effect, making yourself wrong.
When relationships aren't free, they become dull.
They shouldn't be about "you and me" but include everybody.
Otherwise relationships are insular.

The usual way that people relate is "front to front".
That is to say facing each other.
As they try to reach out to the world beyond that person, that
person is always in the way.
This leads to a feeling of being trapped.
If we stand "back to back" (psychologically) we will find that
the other person is always *with* you.
But you are free to express your life with the world, while
always being appropriate to the relationship.
Be *with* someone, not "together but not with them".

RELATIONSHIPS II

Relationship is the most important thing in our lives.

It happens *all* the time, from moment to moment, unless we
avoid it.

Look at your immediate position.

Relationship is a healing process – learning to love
unconditionally.

Any pain or stress means we have not yet achieved
unconditional love.

Conditions might be such as:

"My life is a struggle in relationships, work, money, etc."

"I can't relate. I end up with nobody. I'm always hurt, etc."

"Life is hopeless . . . it's just the same old story"

"The universe is a hostile place – I have to fight for what I
want"

"I can't get what I need".

"There must be something wrong with me".

"Life is a constant upset".

"Love is dangerous".

"I'm not wanted here".

"People hurt me".

"The universe is against me".

A paranoiac thinks the universe is against him.

A mystic thinks it's for him.

All these operating principles and attitudes make relationship
difficult, if not quite impossible.

People cannot get near you.

Explore your own condition.

What is it?

Don't *try* to relate, but be *in* relationship.

I'm in relationship with you already, just dissolve the barrier.

To do this, *be* more.

"Trying" is the way of the mind.

"Being" is much easier.

We cannot avoid relationships with everyone else on the planet.

Relax, and then share yourself with the other person.

Share your Divinity with them.

A relationship is complete when we *feel* love and goodwill.

All those negative conditions are only a mindset.

If your mindset is "No-one loves me", they can't get in.

Once we recognise we are *in* the relationship, the separation
    disappears.

I AM is the *opening* of how people come to me.

The second key is to *see* what our opening is.

Can anyone get through it?

Try "everybody loves me" or "more and more people love me".

With these you dissolve the pattern.

Opening is opportunity.

Like yourself better, so that others can too.

Give yourself love and acknowledgement.

Everyone is our mirror.

We see ourselves in them.

Unconditional love is not "I'll love you if you love me".

I can only change relationships if I change *me*.

Don't add anything – we are *all* loving beings.

We all deserve love and needn't *do* anything more.

Just take away the shackles.

Ask for what you want.

Don't demand, just ask.

Demanding pushes away.

Asking tells others what you want, in case they didn't have their
    aerial up.

Accept what happens.

Having asked, any result is O.K.

We always think we know what is right for another person,
    when the truth is often we do not.

Perhaps we're like the monkey who saved the fish from the river and took it up into the trees as he knew the fish would be safe there.

Take the view there is something good in everything for me.

Love more.

"I love you anyway – no control or binding".

People love to be where they're loved i.e. not controlled.

Tell the truth.

It sets you free.

Lies bind.

Don't *blame* others.

Blame is unwillingness to face your own patterns and to make the inner shifts you need to make.

Be space for each other.

Leave space for the other person to be himself, to grow into his own tree, orchard or garden.

There is only one relationship – the one with yourself.

As we can manage the relationship with ourself, we can relate with everyone.

If not, nothing changes.

Make your own decisions about what you do.

Stop fitting into the pictures of other people – your mother's or father's picture of you – or your mate's.

We are creative beings . . . *Be* creative.

How it is is how you created it.

It will not change until we Think it differently.

If my viewpoint is "it's my father's fault that my life won't work," this makes me the effect of my father.

He runs my life even if dead.

If I am creative, I can restate this.

"I am responsible for my life and I am grateful for my father's input, which I see only as good. It helps me to make my own clear decisions".

It's important that we see parents or authority figures as equals.

They have no better or no lesser viewpoint than ours.

Since it is our life we ultimately must make the choice.

Guilt is the mafia of the mind.

It robs you of joy.

Most people live in guilt and expect to be punished.

Take away the "This is what I should be doing or should not be
    doing".

Do what you choose to do and guilt dies.

To heal guilt, tell the truth about it and forgive.

Rather than live in the attitude "I don't have anything in
    common with other people", look for what you do have in
    common with them.

"What are you interested in?" is the best opening phrase.

"What do you *like* doing?"

Listen with interest.

Use the acknowledgement that "More and more people are
    learning to love me, as I am myself".

Our mental attitudes are intertwined.

Eliminating one starts the cleaning up of the others.

Bring "I am a loving human being" into being.

Don't think about it, *feel* it.

Say it, and become creative.

It makes you radiant and full of beans.

All griping brings the same back to you on the mirror principle.

Express love, and it comes back tenfold.

Give up being right.

It is based on a belief in our programming.

Open up the right brain – express, create, love, dwell in Alpha –
    thus we see things differently.

There is ignorance about soul mates.

Who invented it – Plato?

Where is this one person – this perfect fit?

Where is your soul mate?

It is your own Self.

We look out there for *our* completion of ourself.

The true completion happens within us.

When we are whole, then many people can fit with you.
If you think you're a half, you'll never find the other half.
Why not be a whole looking for another whole that you feel in
    tune with, rather than being a half looking for another
    half?
There aren't any *halves*.
Everyone is whole.
A bad context is: "When I get it together I'll be OK".
Think rather "I'm OK anyway".
The universe works perfectly.
Why are we worrying?
You are already in place, so relax and enjoy rather than strive
    to make it work.
There is no divine meat axe poised over your head – there's no
    God judging you.

We *are* love, and loving is the only valuable thing we do in life.
When I really know who I am, and who you are, love is an
    obvious result.
There are no more obstacles, and we are *love*.

Ask for what you want in a relationship with another person,
    but give that other person the freedom to say "no",
    without getting upset about it, without the other person
    feeling manipulated.
Asking opens the possibilities.
Without asking there is no possibility.
If that person is not willing to grant us our wish, then it is
    surely available elsewhere.

Be careful of ideals, expectations and standards in relationships.
They may ruin your life.
Don't fall in love with a film star image.
It could make you miss the relationship.
It is happening *now*.
Expectations could close your eyes to this.
Standards may set up perfections which no-one could live up to.

Often we impose the image we have of our parents on other
people.
We expect them to live up to it, or not to live up to their
supposed faults.
Forgive your parents.
Do not restrict your field of vision by living in the past.
Don't look for your solutions in the past.
The light that lights your future is here in the present.
Live here.
Do not miss your opportunity.

Instead of dreaming *about* relationships, live *in* them.
"Dreaming about" is not a here and now experience.
It has no creative power.
Living in relationships makes them a present reality.
Create with your thinking the situation you want.
Don't put your attention on trying to eliminate what you don't
want;
That will only make it stronger.
Based on the principle "what we put our attention on
increases", those who have, get more.
Their attention is on having.
Instead of putting your attention on *wanting* a loving
relationship, (which creates more wanting), place your
attention on *having* a loving relationship.
Be grateful for what you have.
This brings more of those things.
Agonising about what you don't have just brings more agony.
Agonising doesn't bring more of what you want.

Most people's idea of a special relationship is based on the idea
"he (or she) is mine".
This is possessive.
Have rather a holy relationship – a "whole" relationship.
This is the viewpoint that we are two free whole beings working
in partnership.
We express our love together in the service of other people.

He (or she) is no longer "mine" as in a "special relationship",
   but a free expression of the Source.

Thinking *about* is philosophy and does not include action . . .
   thus nothing happens.
Thinking about having a bath does nothing.
Having a bath is a creative act and is no longer in the realm of
   thinking *about* it.
It is *thinking* it.
So *think* your relationships, *think* your life.
Don't think *about* them.

Unconditional love is getting *off* any position that stands in the
   way of love.
Mother Teresa sees the face of Jesus in everyone.
See the loving being in everyone.
Call it forth in them and allow them to call it forth in you.

"Time is too slow for those who wait,
too swift for those who fear,
too long for those who grieve,
too short for those who rejoice,
but for those who love time is not"

Henry van Dyke.

HOW TO LISTEN – INTUITION

We have one mouth and two ears.
We should listen twice as much as we speak.

We often don't hear what people are saying.
We are obsessed by our reaction to what they are saying, and
     look within ourselves for a suitable retort.
If you speak, am I *really* hearing what you're saying?
Or am I just reacting to you, trying to outsmart you?
Do I try to present some false facade, entirely missing what you
     are saying or, at least, not acknowledging it?
"There is so much noise in my head, I can't hear a word you
     say."

"Be space" while listening.
Don't react, but allow it to come in as it is said, *then* review it.
Someone might say "I don't like your tie."
Our natural reactive mechanism would be to hear "I don't like
     you".
We would get upset and defend our tie, as if we were defending
     ourselves.
If we give space to the other person and actually *hear* what they
     say, we hear them merely expressing an opinion about the
     tie.
If we allow their opinion into our space, there is no need to
     react or defend anything.
The same can happen in relationships, where an opinion is given
     and it is taken as a personal insult or criticism.
The statement is interpreted before it is really heard.

The highest level of listening is to ourselves.
We often do not listen to the guidance we are receiving within.

Even if we hear it, we often do not act upon it.

Meditation is inner listening.

Your best friend, the wisest person you know and best
counsellor, is your Self.

Dreams are a good way of listening to your Self.

We can build bridges into deeper and deeper levels of our
Selves.

People speak with all of themselves.

Listen not only to what they're saying but to their mannerisms,
presentation and their very essences.

Often what they're saying and the words they use are not the
same.

A person could be saying "I hate you and never want to see you
again" whereas the true communication is "I love you and
I'm upset."

We are all an expression of consciousness.

In tuning into higher levels of our own consciousness, we can
know more fully what people are saying or are going to
say.

The only barriers that there are to listening and to hearing are
those we place there with the mind.

When we dissolve those barriers, we can hear people, even if
thousands of miles away, as if speaking within us.

We are like a radio sender/receiver.

We can tune into people at distance and pick up their
communication.

Sometimes we even hear conversations in our inner ears just as
you might pick up the police on your car radio.

Hearing is a natural faculty, which we can develop through
practise.

Intuition is a natural faculty.

It is a feeling and a knowing not based on past information.

One of the traditional ways of developing intuition is as in
   prayer: the head lowered and looking upwards with the
   closed eyes.
This has the effect of stimulating the third eye and frontal part
   of the brain, which are the sender, and the crown chakra
   and upper part of the brain, which is the receiver.

We often get an immediate impression when we meet someone.
This impression is often an intuitive feeling based on their
   vibration.
It's important that we take notice of this immediate impression,
   as our senses may give us an entirely different impression
   based on how they seem to be.
The mind clouds our intuition with reason.
Reason doesn't know anything other than past conditioning.
Animals are very intuitive.
A dog instantly knows who is friend or foe, though guard dogs
   are trained by man not to listen to their intuition.
Similarly dogs, and often cats, know well in advance when their
   master is nearing home.
By watching the reaction of animals we can be warned or
   taught.

We are our speaking and listening.
If we hear in a filtered, contracted way, we will never know the
   truth.
If we speak in a way that is encouraging, our words uplift.
If we criticise, by making people "wrong", doom and gloom follow.
Just as we are listening, so is the Universe listening.
When "I AM" speaks, the Universe also speaks.
Blind people have a sensitivity of listening to which we should
   aspire.
God is listening – speaking.
When we are truly in touch with our Selves, God is listening,
   God is speaking.
When we *really* listen, we are everybody listening.
Therefore we listen as everyone.

What you put your attention on increases.

With the thought "things could be worse" they get worse.

If you put the whole of your attention on the *now*, your capacity is unlimited.

Most people are in a state of *doing* instead of *being*.

Meeting together allows people to create the right context by *being* together.

We see ourselves separate – but each cell is a hologram of the whole.

Combine yogi and western way of meditation: "Be still and *know* that I Am God."

Spiritual healing means healing your *own* consciousness.

Create the space in which something heals.

Heal the situation in your own consciousness, and the right thinking will turn up, dissolving and healing situations.

Creativity includes creating the new, transforming, reversing a negative situation.

Be.

*Still*ness.

Know (not think or struggle).

I. Am. God (love, source, abundance).

For quick intuition – go "under" into the next state of consciousness (Alpha).

Ask a question.

Make sure you have the right question.

Make the declaration that you already *have* the answer.

Wait until it lands, and then come out of the space (Alpha) and let go of any further concern in the knowledge the answer is on its way.

It arrives at the appointed time – have the expectation of the answer arriving.

Live in the expectation of the answer – a dream, a chance remark of others, words in a book, or intuition.

When we work with intuition, we have an enlarged perspective.

We see health rather than sickness, and this creates the opportunity for health to happen.

The visionary lifts the condition to the vision.

If we see wholeness everywhere, then we invite wholeness.

Hold the vision of friendship or a relationship and then it can
happen.

Practise listening with an uncluttered mind.

Listen in the expectation of an answer – it takes time.

It comes to us eventually, by hearing, seeing or reading the
answer somewhere.

Who we are knows everything long before we ask.

Don't try to make your life work with the reasoning mind –
listen to intuition.

Let go – let God!

A quick way to call on intuition is to imagine yourself headless.

An exercise in intuitive readings is to give immediately your
position in a 1 – 10 reading on any situation – personal
prosperity – personal health – instant answers.

This shows the "nowness" of all thought – the gift is here once
you make the space for it – and if you accept it.

We often reason against our intuitive feelings, to our loss.

Develop the habit of aligning heart and mind with our intuition.

SPIRITUAL HEALING

Spiritual healing is the returning of everything to the One
   Source.
A healing or a "wholing" is a returning to the Oneness of
   everything that has stepped out of there.
Allopathic medicine, herbs, acupuncture, etc., though naturally
   valuable are external applications and come within the
   realm of "doing something to".
Spiritual healing is all-inclusive, and is a working in
   consciousness healing everything – not just bodies, but our
   entire life.
Our life does not come from our dualistic mind.
The disease or condition is spiritualised, losing its destructive
   power and returned to the Source.
This is an act of consciousness, not an act of willpower or a
   result of positive thinking.

There is a fundamental distinction between positive thinking
   and spiritual healing.
Positive thinking acknowledges the presence of disease while
   holding the person in a positive thought structure.
This is effective until the user no longer thinks in a positive
   way, at which time the condition returns.
Spiritual healing deals with the very cause of the condition in
   such a way that it is transformed and no longer exists.
Further, unless this shift in consciousness happens within the
   person being "healed", it is only temporary.
Thus the practitioner of spiritual healing needs not only to
   transform his own consciousness, but that of the patient
   for permanent healing.

Disease has an existence in the physical arena and in the mind, but not in the Self.

In abstract terms, no treatment can heal someone who believes in their sickness.

The healing must come from the deepest level of self.

There are distinctions between physical, mental and spiritual healing.

The medical profession mostly works with physical healing – "You are a body and we'll do something to it to heal it".

This deals with only about 1% of our difficulties.

All parts are related to each other, so it is never just the heart or some single point which is sick.

The belief system about disease has been put in position by someone and we believe it, just as members of a caste in India believe they have higher or lower rank.

Perhaps our belief is entirely wrong, or very substantially limited.

The physical approach is based on trying to change the thing we do or treat the effect without addressing the cause behind it.

Mental healing is still in the dual realm – right and wrong.

Psychoanalysis, psychiatry, mind healing, thought transference, visualising, etc. are all good and work well , but are still in the context of "there's something wrong with you".

The attitude of the practitioner is: "I still have to do something to something which is wrong or bad".

In the Alpha state we begin to get in touch with the Reality of who we are, which the Beta mind does not know.

The Self is not in the mind – it is looking.

So we have to become the observer, the watcher, who knows that it is attachment to the condition that allows its presence.

True healing is to BE with the illness, or the condition in your life which is out of harmony, in such a way that it disappears.

Don't resist it, or ignore it, or try to get rid of it.

By BEING with it, the condition speaks to you.

When you learn from it, it can heal permanently, since all disease is a reminder to us to return to the state of Oneness.

Spiritual healing does not DO anything with the condition, as that gives the sickness energy.

The job of a spiritual healer is very simple – be still (in touch with yourself) and *know*.

Know that there is no separation between you and the Source.

Love, which is who I am, is the healer, not the body or the thought.

That which contains everything and everyone is the healer.

Spiritual healing is healing your own consciousness.

Since there is only one consciousness, it is a question of how we see it.

If a sickness in us disappears, or our perception of a sickness elsewhere disappears, it has the effect of *actually* disappearing in the objective world, unless resisted by whoever is experiencing the condition.

It is naturally someone's free choice to remain sick if they wish to.

In a way we are creating a space in which healing happens.

The situation is healed in our consciousness.

As a result, it finds its right manifestation of wellness.

Although there is only one Self, and God is Good, we live life as if there is a bad, trying to get us.

This possibly came from the guilt that we feel from separating ourselves from the Source – we feel guilty deep down inside.

"If we have something good, we'll have to pay for it later" is a false concept.

If we look for the good in life, we can always find it.

All problems are actually the Self calling for acknowledgement, reminding us not to go into the mind, but into Self.

This seems difficult if we are in the middle of a disease or a
    broken relationship.
The first step is to go into the silence and stillness.
The mind put the problem there in the first place.
For us the problem becomes an opportunity.
It is as if *this* is what we must address for our evolution.
The real drug is not the heroin, but the belief within us which
    holds us from our freedom.
This is a mental drug which can be transformed into a powerful
    and useful energy.
The mind cannot solve its problem because it does not know it
    is drugged.
It needs an act in consciousness to make the shift.
The mind trying to solve its own problems is like a thief going
    to a policeman and saying "There is a thief about" without
    realising himself, that he is the thief.
An expanded view in consciousness, a universal view, is that
    everything that is seemingly without us is really within.
It follows that planetary conditions must be the result of the
    collective thinking of humanity.
Thus, to change the conditions of humanity, an act of
    consciousness is needed which changes the thinking of
    man.
Cleaning up things *outside* of us is only cosmetic and temporary.

The way of thinking until recently was the dependence on
    doctors and authorities to solve our problems for us.
The emerging way is one of personal responsibility in which
    professionals such as doctors become partners and advisers
    in our healing, but *we* take the responsibility.
People who find the key to their sickness can be of great value.
Those who have found the keys in consciousness to, for
    example, cancer or AIDS can make that knowledge
    available to others and become way-showers.
The key to relationships, money and other worldly things is to
    be found within.
Those who find the key can open the door for others.

The starting place is to sit still and know the solution is here at
    hand.
Relax into the Self, which cannot be understood or explained by
    mind.
The Self is only something you can know from experience, not
    from description.
Relax and become that space that contains all.
Realise that everything is here and now.
Realise that joy and happiness is an experience of Self.
If we don't feel it, it is because of incompletion we have with
    the Self.
We are holding it off with a veil of guilt and beliefs in
    something other than the truth of Self.
We must allow ourselves to continue letting go.
We have incompletions in health, money, relationships,
    opinions, evaluations, attitudes, myths, beliefs, two powers
    (duality - god and devil), guilt, karma, death, parents,
    lover, children, family, nation, religion, etc.
All that, plus incompletion in our history, equals our misery.
Incompletion with parents is traumatic and stressful and, for
    most, is one of the more major incompletions.

For many the Christian church, along with other major
    religions, promotes guilt and suffering and thus an
    invitation to bondage in our lives rather than freedom.
There seems to be considerable guilt concerning the disciples
    renouncing Jesus and the crucifixion itself.
The incompletion between Hitler and the Jews is enormous, as
    between Christians and Jews, causing historical stress
    for us.
The Christ is Oneness and knows no guilt and suffering.
Only mind suffers.

In our ignorance of our responsibility to the environment we
    allow its pollution.
This can be considered another incompletion in our state of
    consciousness.

The many stresses which we create in our physical body and in our global body weaken the immune system allowing in such conditions as AIDS, which again is only a reminder.

The solution is not to try harder, but to return to the centre within and surrender to the healing consciousness.

The fear of dying creates stress and disease.

By working in consciousness the fear of death disappears.

Many try to make God work for them i.e., making him Vice President.

Their thinking is "If I pray hard enough, light enough candles, promise suffering, chant enough, do the right mental gymnastics, have the right formula, etc., then God will do what I want".

Fortunately, God does not work for man – or what a mess we would make of things!

Our job is to surrender and allow Him (She or It) to work as us.

In this way healing can truly take place.

The evolution It has in mind can happen.

CLUES TO SELF-HEALING

Most self-healing can be done at Alpha.
At Alpha we know that it is not us who are upset or sick, but
that it is just a mental condition.
Even physical conditions are mental conditions, since matter
cannot be sick.
Alpha is achieved when the brain waves function between 7 and
14 cycles per second.
The Alpha state is a positive state of Presence – not a
disappearance.
There is a positive creation of health, where disease cannot
exist, of love where rejection and resentment cannot exist,
of prosperity where poverty cannot exist.
This is not mental gymnastics, but a conscious creation of a
state of *being*.
No opportunity can be present until we call it into being.
Turn your attention on *health* as a state of being.
Leave no thought or time for unhealth.
Don't think of sickness, worry or fear, until such time as the
state of health is fully Realised in consciousness, and thus
in body.

Where there is still a single healthy part of the body, there is
still opportunity for full recovery.
If the whole body is sick, except for one finger which is well, do
not place attention on the sick body, but rather on the well
finger.
Celebrate the well finger!
Maybe tomorrow you will have *two* well fingers ... and next
week a well hand!
Don't see sickness as an energy and try to knock it out.
That only gives it energy.

It is preferable to encourage health.

The sickness then disappears.

Health *is*, whereas sickness is an imbalance.

When we are out of tune with ourselves, then we are sick.

One of our strongest healing forces is our voice.

Therefore voice (speak) only statements of health, not
   statements of sickness.

Chanting, singing or toning can revitalise the body.

These could be useful in the healing of AIDS and other
   conditions.

The chant U – O – A – E – I refers to strengthening and healing
   all of the seven chakras:[1]

U – 1st and 2nd chakras – root and sexual chakras (security)

O – 3rd chakra – solar plexus centre (upset stomach, anger,
   liver, kidneys)

A – 4th chakra – heart, breast, etc. (love centre – if closed it
   separates the person from love, giving a pain like a
   wounding, and leading towards death)

E – 5th chakra – throat centre (the voice and centre of
   communication)

I – 6th and 7th chakras – pineal gland (third eye) and crown
   chakra (the centre of our vision, receiving spiritual energy,
   I AM).

Sound is very important in healing.

Alpha trainers, biofeedback machines and Alpha sound tapes
   are available on the commercial market.

The Alpha sound tape alone has been said to heal cancer in a
   patient by placing the tape recorder by the diseased leg of
   the patient.[2]

In using Alpha meditations for healing, the following guidelines
   are useful:

– one fifteen minute period a day for general health;

– two fifteen minute periods a day for chronic conditions

– three fifteen minute periods a day for life-threatening
   conditions such as cancer and AIDS;
– some deeply entrenched conditions require conscious dwelling
   in Theta (brain rhythms of between 4 and 7 cycles per
   second).

To get into the Alpha state one system is, with eyes closed, to
   count down inwardly twice.
First visualise "3" three times, then "2" three times and "1"
   three times.
Then, with a feeling of descending in a lift or on a stairway,
   count backwards from 10 to 1.
The experience of Alpha will deepen the more you use it.
Another way of finding this state is to recreate within yourself
   the state of Being you experienced at a time when you felt
   really in tune with yourself.
Return to that essential space.
Each moment is totally creative and every person's experience is
   different.
When you come into a state of Alpha there is a sense of peace,
   a fading of worry and concern, a quieting of the mind and
   a heightening of the senses – particularly of touch and
   hearing.
A telephone ringing is startling when heard in Alpha.

Get the sense of being the space that contains the mind.
The sense that what is going on is in you but not of you.
Feel detachment from the condition (which is not *you*), so that
   you are able to be with it and observe it, without being
   in it.
When doing our Alpha meditation we should adopt a position
   in which the body is comfortable and the back is straight,
   with the head resting comfortably on the shoulders.
Get a feeling of your head being drawn towards the ceiling as if
   on a piece of string.
In Alpha there is a lightening of the density of body weight.

When in the healing Alpha state we can feel the flow of a
    healing energy.

Some thoughts about AIDS:

Sufferers from AIDS should know that they are not bad, not
    wrong.
God (or Whoever) has not condemned you.
Retain total personal self-esteem.
Walk tall, i.e., straight back.
AIDS is a condition, but not *yours* – a smoky room is not *my*
    smoky room.
You are *not* the condition.
You are not the smoky room but yourself.
You don't have AIDS for anything you have done wrong.
If someone gets a disease through which they suffer, they take
    on a condition which the planet has created.
There is no *blame* in AIDS.

The thinking process which has created AIDS is a process which
    has brought us out of harmony with our natural state of
    being.
God is a fulcrum that centres everything.
If something is out of harmony, It will naturally bring that back
    into harmony by requiring people to turn within.
The AIDS breakout requires people to look within, where
    doctors cannot help.
Those with the condition will do the hardest looking – their
    intent is greater.
They are doing this looking for the world and are thereby
    becoming heroes.
They are the ones who are showing the way.
Public opinion will turn around to take an interest in the
    solutions they find.
Public respect will follow.

AIDS sufferers have a particular job to do in finding the key in
consciousness to this personal and global issue.
It is an important step in the evolution of the planet.
They are the pioneers and light-bringers in this issue.
Condemning them will not help.
Let us respect and support them in finding the solution.
If AIDS patients begin to feel that they are pioneers in this era
of the planetary evolution, their self-esteem and enthusiasm
will return.
It is they who may discover not only how to recreate the
immune system, but many other things besides.
Self-healing is the joyful work of returning everything to the
Oneness of Divine Being.

[1] The author was introduced to this Chant by Jill Purce
[2] This claim was made to the author by Jose Silva of Silva Mind Control. The author
also acknowledges that the essence of the information in this section is the result of
research by Jose Silva and his organisation who also manufacture Alpha trainers and
biofeedback machines.

THE CHAKRAS

Our words create our capacities.
"I can" or "I can't" fix what we can do.
Using "I can" we open ourselves.
Hear only good.
Speak only good.
Good is an opening – it leads lifewards.
If we live in the openings the chakras open.
If we resist and live in the closings, "can't", "won't",
    "shouldn't", etc., the chakras close and we move
    deathwards.
The chakras are energy centres.
They open as our consciousness in them is liberated.
If we dwell in negative experiences or generate negative thought
    forms, we close the chakras down.

The lower chakra centres are at a lower frequency and rise to
    the crown centre.
The crown centre is the highest physical body centre and runs at
    the highest frequency.
We can transform a low frequency to a higher one and we can
    bring a high frequency into a lower one.
The heart centre is the love centre and the centre of the chakras.

If we can raise the lower centres up to and through the heart,
    then we will only create loving vibrations.
If we raise the heart up through the throat and mind, we will
    only speak and think loving thoughts and words.
If we bring frequencies of a higher consciousness down into the
    lower chakras, we can spiritualise them.
Ultimately we can change their form, raising the body to a
    higher manifestation.

In order to effect these transformations we need to take responsibility.
Live from the centre of our Being.
Don't be seduced into believing in the subjective world as the source of our well-being.
The latter approach brings only misery and fear.

There is no such "thing" as a chakra.
They are energy centres within a state of being.
The idea of them having physical positions in the body is actually incorrect.
There are many mind centres in the body.
In fact, each cell is a mind centre.
The chakras are major mind centres which store experience.
By working with the chakras in healing applications the body can be revitalised.
Limiting thought patterns can be released from the body.
The chakras can be liberated to their proper function.
Awareness of the holding of tensions in the chakras enables us to release the holding and free up our life.
Useful assistance can be given in this work with intuitive massage.

Some aspects of the work of the chakras:

The root chakra at the base of the spine is the centre for the legs.
The root chakra roots us into the earth.
It is also the centre of the generative organs.
Earth energy enters through the root chakra and the feet.

The second chakra is the Kath or Hara, the lower emotional centre.
This creative sexual centre expresses through the generative organs.
It is in this centre that the baby is created.

It is the powerhouse, hence Tai Chi's focus on it for their
power.
It is the security centre, so it gives the sense of being secure and
safe in life.
It deals with the organs near it, the intestines, womb. etc.

The third chakra is the solar plexus centre, the higher emotional
centre.
Here all upset is experienced.
Anger is linked with the liver and kidneys.
An upset stomach or intestines generally has an emotional base.

The fourth chakra is the heart centre, the centre of love.
Pain felt there is the pain of separation from love.
The heart centre is the highest emotional centre and is the
centre of the person.
The use of heart energy to transform can occur when, if angry
with someone, we raise the anger from the solar plexus into
the heart.
This transforms anger into compassion.

As the heart centre is in the middle, energy flow can be
managed in both directions, upwards and downwards.
It is therefore important that the heart centre be open or the
individual will always be in stress and will not function
well.
The pain of separation that is felt can often be life-threatening,
like the deep wounding that is felt when a loved one dies.
In these cases work must be done to heal the heart and restore
it to its open and healthy state.
The physical parts of the body influenced by the heart centre
are the heart, breast, lungs, etc.

The fifth chakra is the throat centre, the second creative centre.
We create with our voice, the centre of communication.
It is the first centre of which we have *conscious* control.
It is the centre of our speaking and listening.

89

It is important that we take responsibility for the way we speak
and the way we listen.

If we suppress, withold, bottle up or swallow our feelings – if
we lie or withhold the truth – then the throat centre is
affected and problems occur in that area.

The physical organs the throat chakra affects include the lungs
throat, mouth and ears.

The sixth chakra is the third eye – the pineal gland.

It is the centre of imagination, intuition, intellect, determination
and vision among other aspects.

This is the centre of thinking, where the eye is single.

The sixth chakra is largely responsible for the eyes.

When the pineal gland is opened, it stands erect and can receive
and radiate spiritual energy.

With its opening the connection is made with the seventh centre.

Spiritual energy is able to flow down the spine.

The seventh centre, the crown chakra at the top of our head,
opens to the heavens.

Spiritual energy enters through the crown.

It is the I AM.

Here the human connects with the higher states of being beyond
the human state.

THE MIRROR PRINCIPLE

What we see in the world is a mirror of ourself.
From the Oneness the Self looks through the filter of the mind.
All that we see is a creation of the mind.
Be not only the observer, but the observed and the observing.
The mind pigeonholes and puts things into these three separate
     places, but they all come from the same source and are
     mental positions in the same space.
The mirror principle is demonstrated practically in the way
     people respond to us.
They reflect our state of consciousness.
That which is over "there" reflects the way I am perceiving.
If I feel people criticise me, reject me and misunderstand me,
     that is a direct reflection of the way I feel about myself.
If I see only hopelessness, enemies, aggression and problems,
     this is how the world will reflect to me.

A dangerous position is "I'm right".
If we're always trying to be right, then we get upset with people
     who do not agree with our opinions or our solutions.
It is a great release giving up being right and defending
     positions.
Instead of getting angry with people who don't agree with us, or
     who challenge us in some way, we can be grateful to them
     for revealing our mental attachments and allowing us to
     acknowledge the truth of who we are.
All the things we react to in our partners are aspects of
     ourselves which we need to clear up.
In that sense our partners are perfect for us, as they directly
     reflect what we need to learn.

When we accuse people we accuse ourselves and reveal the low
quality of our attitudes.

When we point one finger at a person, there are three pointing
back at us.

If I accuse you of being selfish, it awakens me to my own
selfishness.

Only a selfish person sees selfishness.

If we turn the "you" of our accusations into "I" and then make
the same statement, it is very revealing.

"My husband rejects me" becomes "I reject me".

When we can see the truth in the mirror, we can do something
about it.

The people who are irritating and annoying you become your
teachers.

If you don't react to someone's upset (criticisms, annoyances,
etc.), then it probably does not apply to you.

The next stage would be to eradicate it as a condition at a
global level.

Being personally free of cancer is one thing, but the total
eradication of cancer on the planet is another thing.

Use the mirror principle at various levels: private, family, social,
business, national, global, etc.

By working in my own consciousness, in my own body, I can
work towards the healing in the reflection, in the world.

People always look outside of themselves when they are upset
and put the blame on someone or something else.

Turn inwards and heal your own state of consciousness.

This is done by becoming more aware of thoughts and emotions
that we hold on to.

Work in consciousness to free ourselves of them.

Ultimately I am not free until everyone is free.

I am not free of an addiction, a disease or a condition of any
sort, until its very existence has disappeared, and everyone
is free of it.

So long as prejudice exists in one person, the world is not free
of it, and nor are you or I.
As we all come from the same Source and are perpetually
linked, an understanding of the mirror principle becomes
fundamental in the understanding of human relationships.

When we desire something externally, it is a belief that we are
separated from the thing that we desire.
When we heal the desire within ourselves, and acknowledge that
what we want is here already waiting to express, we have
healed our belief in separation.
We have started the creative process.
Dwell in the Presence that contains all things.
Work with this consistently both in meditation and in your
daily life.
It is this process that does the work.

The mirror naturally reflects our positive aspects as well.
When we are generous, loving, supportive and open, the world
will reflect this.
If I acknowledge people, I am acknowledged.
If I am enthusiastic, people around me are enthusiastic.
When I give, I am given to.
Don't expect your good to be necessarily reciprocatcd from the
individual you gave to.
Often people shower love on one person and are disappointed
when this love does not appear to be reciprocated.
The love may well be returned from another person or from a
group of people.
This is how it is mirrored.

Genuine gifts of love, money, time, acknowledgement, etc.
return in their own time and multiply.
Notice the way you feel when making the gift.
When giving money, it is important to feel prosperous.
Then the world will mirror prosperity.
If you feel loss, then the world will mirror loss.

The mirror is always the same.
It reflects only from your state of consciousness.
It is neither fair nor unfair.
It is simply a mirror.
If we always see the good in everything and in every individual,
then good is mirrored to us and life has a magical quality.
Most people criticise, dwelling in the negative, which only
mirrors back the same.

Dealing with duality:
— Though we see twoness, we can always realign it in our
thinking and see only oneness
— Instead of seeing good or bad, we can come from Oneness,
the knowledge that ultimately all is Good.
— We will look for Good and see Goodness everywhere, by-
passing the mind's opinions.
— Instead of seeing an inner world and an outer world, we see
only one world.
— That which is seemingly outside us becomes inside us.
— That which is seemingly inside us – our thoughts – becomes
as much outside us, all at the same time.
This requires a quantum leap in the way we perceive.
It is not being more intelligent or more apt at doing it a certain
way.
It is perceiving from an entirely different space.
It is useful to develop a mental mechanism or habit, that
whenever we see twoness, we automatically correct to
oneness.
Instead of saying "There is God and there is me" (twoness),
restate it as "God as me".
If the truth of this were fully acknowledged, many people's
religious and spiritual difficulties would be ended.
As God expresses as me, then the truth is that love, health, life,
joy and prosperity express as me.
The question is "to what extent do I acknowledge that and call
that expression into being?"

Working from the outside is a patch-up job, cosmetic at the best
of times.
Go within.
Acknowledge the truth of Being, from where the fundamental
change is made, and healing brought about.
There is no separation between inner and outer worlds.
There only seems to be 'Beingness'.
There is only I AM, only God – the biggest mirror of all.
Look always into the face of God.
See Its reflection everywhere.

GRATITUDE

Gratitude is the great attitude.
To take a negative view on things and the world has the effect
of closing you down.
Watch your body.
When you are taking a negative stand or feeling some sort of
loss, depending on which negative stand you take, you
close down an appropriate part of your body.
For example, a sexual rebuff might result in sexual impotence.
Emotional upsets might lead to stomach ulcers.
Spiritual training recreates the flow throughout the body and
opens any of the closed chakras.
Gratitude (coupled with forgiveness) is the great healer.
When dwelling in gratitude, we begin to see the gift that is
present in what we originally thought was a loss or a
disadvantage.

If my mother dies, the normal reaction is grief and a deep sense
of loss, as if I have been cut off from love.
This naturally closes the body.
By dwelling in gratitude and in the knowledge that love is
always present, my grief is short lived.
I acknowledge a greater love.
I become aware that my mother is in an expanded state of
consciousness, in a place that is good for her.
If I lose my job, instead of being upset about it and putting
myself down, I dwell in gratitude for the opportunity to
take the next step in my life, to reach for higher horizons.
If I get sick, I avoid resenting it.
I avoid trying to defeat the disease, as if it were an enemy.

Instead I dwell in the gratitude that I will be able to
    acknowledge that the condition is a gift, leading me to new
    solutions within myself.
It will raise my state of consciousness and put me in a better
    position for the years ahead.
When the conscious shift is made, the disease disappears.

It is important to generate gratitude for love, health, prosperity,
    life, etc., even when the mind does not agree and cannot
    see anything to be grateful for.
Continue being grateful and the way opens.
If you have resentment for an individual, dwell in gratitude.
That person is showing you yourself, giving you the opportunity
    to clean your attitudes.
Love is the space that we are.
We don't have to find it.
We are it.
Gratitude is a form of prayer.

On praise
O, tell us, poet, what do you do?
    I praise
But the deadly and violent days
how do you undergo them, take them in?
    I praise
But the namelessness – how do you raise
that, involve the unnameable?
    I praise
What right have you, through every phase,
in every mask, to remain true?
    I praise
– and that stillness and the wild affray
know you, like star and storm?
    Because I Praise

Rainer Maria Rilke

The highest form of prayer is praise – not "asking" for things.
It is dwelling in gratitude for the love of God.
Prayer to something or someone is dualistic and sees God as
    external to you.
A prayer with "Please, God..." is immature and, in a way,
    ridiculous.
It stops God being a part of you.
Rather acknowledge Its Presence and listen.

Forgiveness is giving up our attitudes about something that was
    or was not done.
"I give up my attitude that you wronged me."
"I give up my attitude that you rejected me or took what was
    mine."
The result is that I have released the supposed wrong, and love
    and harmony return.
Naturally, I must also forgive myself.
Once we acknowledge that all is God's love and God's working,
    forgiveness is the natural consequence leading to a new
    peace and well-being.
Once we forgive, gratitude returns.
One leads to the other.

AFFIRMATIONS

Affirmations are statements we create and use for our
well-being.

If we do not consciously create positive affirmations, we find
ourselves stuck with affirmations presently in our
consciousness.

Most of these are not useful, and are detrimental to our
wellbeing.

By making an affirmation we create a potential.

By dwelling in this potential, for example "I am prosperous",
we are acknowledging our source of being.

We remind ourselves to live within that context.

When we make an affirmation it tends to bring up the
negatives, in the consciousness, to that statement.

When I say "I am prosperous" the mind throws up "No you're
not! You're broke, etc."

This is useful, because we now know the statements in mind we
need to transform.

Affirmations are best said aloud with conviction for a few
minutes in front of a mirror.

The important thing is to say them (or write them) until you
feel the truth of them.

When we write them, write the affirmation and record the
negative reactions to it.

Keep writing the affirmation, and turning around the negative
reactions until the mind accepts the affirmation.

Be the source of your own affirmations.

Use your own voice, rather than listen to affirmations recorded
by others on tape.

This tape accustoms your mind to accept the affirmations of
another voice, which is contrary to personal sovereignty.

Practise affirming on a daily basis.

Just doing it once or twice is usually not enough.

It is a matter of transforming the thoughts in our mind.

It is not so much the affirmation that is important, since it is not mind that makes the change, but Spirit.

Affirmation leads to Realisation.

Give yourself permission to affirm the things that you want.

Check that what you want is in no way detrimental to anyone else.

Affirmation is the first step in creating a new direction in life.

Use your affirmations to improve yourself, not to compete with others.

An affirmation on forgiveness could be "I forgive everyone in my past, present and future".

A useful affirmation in all situations, whether good or supposedly bad, is "only good can come from this".

This will dissolve crisis and panic.

It is a context which pulls for a positive result.

In our vision we can see anything.

Thus we can create whatever affirmations we choose.

We can create affirmations for health, love, prosperity, career, purpose, etc.

We can call forth Self, Music, Laughter, Love and any other positive experience.

The law of increase: What you put your attention on increases.

With the thought "Things are getting worse" they get worse.

We experience the Biblical quote "What I most feared has come upon me".

Similarly the Thought "life is so good to me" or "I lead a charmed life" brings that result.

If we put our whole attention on the Now our capacity is unlimited ... every cell is listening.

If we send messages saying "Give up", the cells do.

If we send messages of encouragement, the cells respond.

Since affirmation is only a stepping stone to Realisation, we
    must bring the Presence of Being to our words.
It is this that gives them the power.
We can use affirmation to unravel the hypnotism of the
    dualistic worlds.

The more useful way to use willpower is for holding a context,
    to hold the space or the Reality of our affirmation as being
    true.
Allow Spirit to fill the space.
People grow old when they stop creating context and settle for
    their present condition.
It is a service to others to have what you want in life.
It harms no-one.
A powerful and simple context is "God alone is here".
If we don't programme our minds others will.
Most of our programmes are self-negating statements.
If we don't change them, we cannot expect our lives to change.

George Bernard Shaw said that the only thing that separated
    him from other people was that he used the creative power
    of Thought about three times a week, whereas most other
    people never used it at all.

Clear thinking is:
I want this.
I see myself having it.
I commit myself to its manifestation.
I plan how I am going to manifest it.
I surrender the creation and trust the process, holding firm to
    my affirmation.

(See also "How to Use Your Dreams")

THE GROUP CONSCIOUSNESS

Since there is only oneSelf, whatever I look at is mySelf.
With the eyes (of division) I see other people.
But I really see mySelf expressed in different forms.
When I look from misery, jealousy and sickness, I will see that
    everywhere.
When I look from Love, Freedom and Health, I will see that
    everywhere.
When a group of people come together and I view it from the
    oneSelf, rather than being separate individuals, they form a
    completion of me.
We're so used to thinking of "me" that we tend to see "them"
    as "others" rather than as expressions of the same
    "I-ness".
When a group of people come together, the power is a
    multiplication.
When twelve people are aligned, the power is not twelve times
    the power of one, but, maybe, one hundred and forty four
    times.
Furthermore, in this power our limiting characteristics are
    transcended, with the possibility of being transformed.

The value of the group consciousness, such as spiritual study
    groups and work groups, is not so much the content,
    what's being talked about, what's being done, but what
    each person is experiencing.
If you are having a particular reaction, then explore that
    reaction.
If you are lifted, go with the experience.
In a group there is a Presence working as a catalyst.
We can experience this Presence and feel it.
It is much stronger than when we are working individually.

When leading a group, always talk to the group consciousness.
By talking to the group consciousness all the questions and
    needs in the room are attended to, and you do not need to
    know, as leader, the specific needs of individual members
    of the group.
Allow the Presence to bring the solutions and act as a vehicle of
    that Presence.
The Presence goes beyond all the knowledge in the group.
It reaches into the Source of Knowing.
It can serve all members in the appropriate way.

When we raise our state of consciousness, the world changes
    naturally.
This means we do not have to go out and "change" the world,
    since our efforts will be in vain until we have changed
    ourselves.

Thoughts are like fish in water.
They flow through consciousness.
They do not belong to you or me.
We merely attach to them as if they do.
We can stand and watch them and use those that are useful.
Unless we are vigilant in watching the prevailing thoughts that
    are around us, we can easily be sucked into mass thinking,
    or the thought patterns of others.
This is not necessarily beneficial for us.
If we allow other people to do our thinking for us, or to
    dominate us with their thoughts, we lose our sovereignty.
It is important to be sovereign in our thinking, and only to
    align with a group consciousness if we are in agreement
    with it.

MEDITATION

There is nothing weird in meditation.
Convoluted techniques for meditation are not necessary.
The essence of meditation is fundamental to the Centre, which
　　holds the vision of Oneness.
We come from the Centre, the Sovereign Being and Oneness
　　　- we return everything to Oneness.
Duality is part of the Oneness.
We don't deny duality - it has its existence in the world of
　　duality.
It is *in* the Oneness that we explore and experience duality
　　　- no separation.

Meditation is dwelling in the Oneness.
The only place that you can dwell in the Oneness is at the level
　　of meditation.
When we are in a state of meditation, we are in a state of
　　Alertness.
When we are in the Alpha state of meditation, we are more
　　alert than in the eyes-open awake state, which isn't usually
　　alertness, because the mind is spinning.
We are in the mind plane, with the eyes-open state.
In meditation we observe the mind plane.
We become the observer, the knower, the watcher.
We watch the mind play - we watch thoughts coming and going.

People tend to hang on to thoughts -'These are *my* thoughts',
　　watching 'my' mind.
There is no 'my' mind to watch.
If you observe, from your place of meditation, thoughts come
　　and thoughts go - what makes them 'yours' ?
Why do you need to hold on to them ?

Why need to get involved with them?
Why not just let them go?
Let them pass.
When you do this, a shift comes, and you feel alert, present,
    and aware.
Dwell in that place.
This is meditation.

The whole purpose of all the techniques which people write
    about - Buddhists and others - is to get you to that place.
That place is of Oneness, of Alertness, of Being the Knower.
We can let go of all the techniques, once we know that the
    purpose is to be Alert.
Meditation is the whole of life being Alert - living the life of
    Alertness.

Being a meditator does not mean to simply close your eyes and
    look into space.
A meditator dwells in the alert state in every part of the day.
His/her life is about becoming totally conscious, becoming
    totally aware.
Everybody, more or less, is a meditator - often without
    knowing it.
Going to sleep and waking up we are in a state of meditation.
We could not survive otherwise.
If we weren't at the Alpha and Theta level at some time, we
    could not survive.

Where we can score is in becoming conscious meditators - using
    this facility.
We develop our nervous system to be able to take far greater
    charge, awakening genius.
More and more of the cosmic energy is available to us.
More and more we find that our whole system changes and is
    transformed.
It must not be sporadic, but regular, like cleaning our teeth
    or eating.

105

It is probably the single most valid aspect of the work.

Be able to be still and to watch thoughts.
Learn how not to get involved with thoughts that you don't
    want to get involved with .
Learn to be separated from the thinking that is going on.
Meditation is something which we should all spend more time
    developing as part of our lives.
We work from the outside in, trying to change things, but
    nothing changes.
When the change is only a shift in mind, it will not last - like
    shifting furniture.
For a fundamental shift, we must go to that place where the
    shift can take place.
The shift takes place as an act of Awareness.
The mind has to let go and surrender to that state of
    Awareness.
Awareness brings the shift.

When we sit down to meditate, we may need to key in.
Use any key which you find useful - 'God alone is here', 'I am
    eternally present'.
You can also use alignment with Christ, or the Buddha, or
    another similar figure which gives you a lift.
If you want to work with a particular subject in your meditation
    - health, prosperity, love, or relationships, then use a key
    which aligns with the statement.
'I am an eternal prosperous being' or 'Prosperity for all'
    awakens the wealth that you are.

'I am Divine Being', 'I am ageless beauty', 'ageless health',
    or whatever you find brings you into that sense.
'I am divine life', 'I am the daughter of love'.
Work with keys such as these until the sense comes, and then
    you don't need the words.
Thus you get through what the mind and thoughts have to say
    to the Truth that is behind.

If there is some specific thing you are working with, there will
be a feeling of release when it is done
- you will *know*.
In effect you return the thought to the Oneness, you return it to
the whole in a creative way.
You are not going backwards, but moving forwards.
You are mastering the ability to transform the physical
condition.
The work which you are engaged in is to come from the
spiritual wholeness, and to transform the physical
condition, the mental condition, the emotional condition in
such a way that it is raised up to that state of meditation.

Meditation is a powerful way of living.
People who use it on a regular basis find that their lives begin
to change naturally, that their creativity improves (writers,
musicians, etc.).
In meditation you dwell in the Self - you don't need to achieve
anything.
One experience in meditating is - if someone is being abusive,
they stop being abusive - if they don't stop, they disappear
from our life.

Meditation is an active state - not passive.
It's a force that is rising.
You become clearer on what you want, you become naturally
assertive and dynamic.
You don't need to engineer it, or put it together, or go in and
hammer the table!
Your whole being asserts itself.
You're clear on what you want.
You need no negatives.

When people are abusive to us, it is because we have that
negative in us.
The world mirrors us.

Whatever is happening to us, we know is going on in our own
   consciousness.
Don't make other people wrong - look at our own
   consciousness to see why we attract this sort of response.
What is doing this?
Why is our life this way?
We created it out of our thinking.
We need to shift that thinking for our lives and relationships to
   change.

The way to change our thinking is to observe it as a mirror.
So we meditate - see what it is, and release it.
I feel insecure, so people make me feel insecure, putting me
   down.
I rip myself off, so I find people in life rip me off.
I blame them for it, but in actual fact I'm inviting it.
My statement is 'Please rip me off'.
Once we have unshackled all this, we find that we state
   what we want.
Natural assertion will come from meditation - not wimpishness.
'Natural assertiveness' means you won't need to assert yourself,
   you'll just relate.

When you're in meditation, you can see what's pulling you -
   whether it's an emotional pull, a heart pull.
You can feel it in the system.
You just sit there, and don't do anything.
Just be with it in such a way that it begins to clear in the
   system.
It is a purification process - you observe how the mind works in
   that system.
As we keep purifying the system, and changing the nervous
   system, we find that we will naturally fall in line with the
   way that our lives should go.
Don't try to force it in a way that is not the direction in which
   we can best express ourselves.

My sense is to meditate frequently - sometimes just for ten
   minutes.
If an upset, or attachment comes up, sit down and meditate on
   it for ten minutes - even while you're on the bus.
It is sometimes useful to set a period aside for longer
   meditation, but it is not obligatory.
What works for you is the right way.
Lunchtime - before you go to bed - just after rising, use *your*
   way of doing it.

Ultimately you are always operating from the Oneness - like a
   permanent meditation.
You achieve a permanent state of awareness and alertness, and
   so are not involved with the mental drama.
If you step out of conversation inwardly, and just step into the
   Oneness, the conversation often sounds just like a couple
   of old ducks quacking.
It has nothing to do with struggling to make the world work.

When you are involved with the conversation, trying to get your
   point across, it is very meaningful, but in meditation you
   step out of the meaning of the words, in the knowledge
   that the thoughts you have had are of no value.
There is no peace in the functioning of the mind - only stress.
The mind is opposites trying to balance themselves.
Meditation *is* the balance - the centre.
That is where people should look for peace of mind.

When you complete something there is space, and in the space
   comes creation.
If you want to create something, make sure that there is a space
   available for it.
If you find that your creativity is blocked, it means something is
   incomplete.
If your life is blocked, something is incomplete.
The same with relationships.

If you find a point of completion and enjoy the pause, you
 might get a brilliant idea coming through which you didn't
 think of.
It might take you in a whole different direction, or double your
 business in a week.
If ideas come to you, they are like god children.
Write them down, and give those away which are not directly
 useful to you.
By writing down the ideas which come to you in meditation,
 you train the consciousness to throw up good ideas.
Good ideas are creative, make the world go round, and even
 make money!

The Bible says 'seek me early in the morning' - a good time to
 meditate.
Meditate when the energy is high - over the lunch period is
 often a marvellous time to meditate.
Alertness is not a mentally active state : by alertness I mean
 a Presence.
I am Hearing, Seeing, Being - I'm very finely tuned, very
 sensitive.
If someone walked in the door a hundred yards away, I would
 hear it.
It is a super sensitiveness - but you are not mentally involved.
Some people escape in meditation - they disappear - but it is
 important to be Present.
Go to that place where you take your mental turmoil, and
 transform it.
So when you come back, it isn't there.
Your attachment to the problem disappears.
You may still not have the money to pay the bills, but you are
 no longer agonising about it.
The creative act of writing is dwelling in the state of creativity -
 like a state of meditation.
Not only are you dwelling in the alertness, but also producing,
 operating at high levels.

Transcending in meditation is not enough - we have to
    transform.

The only purpose of a mantra is a key - in to the Self.
Once you have keyed into the self, why do you need a mantra?
On the other hand chants, vowels which open the chakras, are
    something different
Chanting uses the sound current to create waves and open the
    centres.
Even then, you end up in silence.
The sounds, running up through the chakras are :
    U - O - A - E - I.
(See Clues to Self Healing).
Go through them, and even use them the other way round.
Play with them.
After chanting yourself down, be still, and be aware, and watch
    your thinking.
They are not your thoughts - they are thoughts.

So in your meditation, remember, you are the Knower.
In that state of I AM, you dwell in the Oneness.
From the state of Oneness, watch thoughts as they arise.
They come and they go.
Let them pass.
Remain alert.
Rest in that state of Divine Being - the state of Immortal bliss.
It is in this state that you truly Know who you are.
You touch the nature of your Being.
The wholeness, the vastness that you are.
It is here that you know that you are Infinite Love, Immortal
    Life, Peace, Prosperity, Health.
This is your true being.
All we need to do is to let go of our belief in anything other
    than that.
We need to surrender our limited thinking.

Let the sense of joy - this energy - permeate your whole Being.
Radiate from the very centre.
So you lose all awareness of being a separate entity.
You become the vastness Itself.
Nothing is separate from you.
This is the place that all people seek, and few know where to
    find it.
It is here that we can dwell in the vision of Oneness.
God alone is, Love alone is.
There is nothing outside of that.
So you can truly relax and let go of the tensions and stress.
Just watch anything mind has to say, and don't get involved.
Be still, and know that you are the Divine Presence Itself.
There is no superior God.
You are That.

AMARAM HAM
MADHURAM HAM
I am Immortal
I am Blissful

*This lecture and "The Spiritual Dimension" were given at the Centre in Battersea,
London, Spring 1988.

NB. The author acknowledges Swami Shyam of the International Meditation Institute in
Kullu, India, for his guidance in the principles of meditation.

THE SPIRITUAL DIMENSION

We should certainly explode the idea of spirituality and
    materiality as being separate.
They are all one and the same thing.
We have to give up our separatist thinking.
So we don't see this is "spiritual", this is "material" — it is all
    spirit.
Material and spirit are in the final count synonymous.
The new "Superstring" theory illustrates the level at which all
    the dimensions, nine of them, unite.
Superstrings are unimaginably small.
They are 10 to the 20th power smaller than protons.
The theories describing them reconcile the conflict between the
    quantum theory and the theory of relativity.
The superstring theory transforms our ideas about space and
    time.[1]

There is only the tiniest particle of matter for infinite space.
Why are we so matter conscious?
The Truth is everything is Spirit.
What we need to do is to enrol matter in its spirituality.
So we transform the condition of the physical so that it becomes
    spirit.
How does this change the world?

We have always been trying to get into heaven, get *out* of here
    into heaven.
It is the Christian, Muslim and Buddhist base.
All religions use "We're in this base, and we have to get to
    another base called heaven".

[1] The Superstring theory is described at length by Michael B. Green in the Scientific
American, September 1986, pages 44 to 56.

113

This gives endless striving, plus the concept that the spiritual
   dimension is the right place and the physical dimension is
   the wrong place.
They teach that we must get out of the physical dimension —
   that we must become enlightened, get into nirvana or get
   realised, to get away from this bad physical place.
They teach that to be material, or to put attention on material
   things, is wrong.
This has been the half-baked thinking for thousands of years.
It is based on the premise that there are two places, one is right
   and one is wrong.
It is based on the premise that the heavenly place is good and
   the worldly place is bad.
It is based on the premise that there is somewhere to go anyway
   — all in duality.
It is based on the premise that there is somewhere to get to, and
   not that we're it already.

The truth is — IT IS.
Life IS.
There's nowhere to "get to".
There's no superpower god that lives separate from us.
There is no more god than you and I.
It exists as our consciousness, our state of Being.
It explodes a whole lot of theories.
It wipes out the whole religion game.
It wipes out all of the "get better" programmes.
In one go we realise that there is only Here.
Here is all of it.

Who I am is already Realised!
There is nothing to Realise.
I am It already.
It is not a question of I am a human being in potential and in
"This seed is a potential tree".
This is not so because a seed IS *tree*.
A tree is.

114

Nothing is in "potential" — it is just that our vision is faulty.
We don't see tree, because we look with the eyes of division,
and the eyes of becomingness, not with the eyes of Being.
The eyes of Being see "tree", "human being", they don't see
separate individuals.
They see human beingness, "I", the One Self.
The eye of Oneness *sees*.
It is the eye of twoness which sees separation, yesterday and
tomorrow, right and wrong.
With the eye of twoness we get caught in suffering, with good
and bad, god and devil.

So there is no spirit *and* matter — they are both the same thing.
If we look from the space of Oneness, then they are together.
People who are trying to become spiritual are materialists.
They are bound to matter.
The joke is that people who call themselves "spiritual" are also
bound to matter, because they are trying to get out of it.
The truth is that we need to get *into* matter, because it is in
matter that we will find freedom.
It is through matter that we will find the key.
That is the step that mankind now needs to make.
People have tried the "getting-out game" and it is a cul-de-sac.
The way is to explore the heights and the depths together.
The way out is the way in!

Only mind has cause and effect, from the ultimate space there is
no cause and effect.
We have so many laws drilled into us — what goes up must
come down, what's born must die.
We just accept it — but it is only the law because we believe it.
We have made it solid with our thinking.
There is a story about the tribe which thought that the world
ended at the edge of their wood.
If they came to the edge of the wood, they couldn't see beyond
the edge of the wood.

115

If you stepped beyond the edge of the wood, they couldn't see
you.
Their thinking condition said that the world ended at the end of
the wood.

How many edges of the wood have we got in our thinking?
How many things have we accepted as true, so that we don't
look beyond it?
We have to be totally alert to the limitations we place upon
ourselves.
Our tendency is to blame the conditions of our life, and we
don't look in our own selves to see where the end of the
wood is.
What limitations have we created?
My definition of madness is expecting the world to change
without changing our self.
We see people like that all the time, desperate because the world
doesn't change.
Their personal world doesn't change — "I can't get the things
in the world that I want".
So they try harder, do different things, and more things, but
they don't change *themselves*.
They don't change their state of consciousness, release some of
the limited thinking that they have, and move the edge of
their wood.

The whole principle of working with vision is to lift the
possibility.
When you come up to a limitation in your thinking, create a
new vision.
Go beyond your wood to a whole continent, an ocean and
further.
It is all possible.
There is no cause and effect, only thought structures in our
thinking.
We put the thought structures there, we are infinite, so create
something new.

If you notice that you have a recurring pattern of behaviour,
heal your mind loop.

We find ourselves in mind loops.

We think "I've done something here, and my life's wonderful,
I'm off on this whole new trip" and then suddenly you find
yourself back where you started.

In fact it was just a bigger loop.

It can be on a daily, monthly or ten yearly cycle, even a
lifetime.

If after a ten year cycle you end up where you started, you ask
"What's the point? I always end up in the same place".

To be able to get out of the mind loop, the first thing is to
identify the loop.

Reincarnation is a mind loop.

It's the belief in life and death.

If you are hooked into thinking of reincarnation as a reality,
then your loop is just that.

Some spiritual teachings say "get off the cycle of birth and
rebirth" — the way to get off this wheel is to recognise
that it's a mind loop.

Since I'm all and everything, what reincarnates?

The idea is just an attachment.

All that reincarnates is who I think I am — that's all.

It is just a mind loop!

I get out of it by recognising it, and *being with* the condition
until it dissolves as a reality.

Breakthrough is when you are hitting up against the top of a
mental limitation, and instead of letting it win, you stay
with it, alert in consciousness, until you suddenly find that
you're through it.

In that moment you take away the energy of the limitation, and
it doesn't have the same power over you.

The whole functioning of the mind is to hold in place our belief
systems.

117

It is a survival machine, responsible for the preservation of our
    thoughts about who we are and are not.
The Self does not need preserving.
It already Is.

If we have created an entity which is separate from Self,
    separate from Deity, separate from God, then the mind's
    job is to preserve that entity.
It does this with all the thoughts and beliefs that you have
    given it.
Once you surrender the thoughts and beliefs, the mind's job is
    over in that sense.
It can become more of a servant, to express the infinite wisdom
    that we are.
If you take away someone's belief, they go crazy (by saying
    "God doesn't exist", for example), because they're left with
    looking at the truth.
The mind does not want to do that, because it is based on that
    belief.
It is very shaking to realise that you are operating on a belief
    that is actually inaccurate.
If you have the courage to be with it, you achieve breakthrough.
For example "My goodness, I've been basing my life on the
    belief that there's somewhere to get. My whole life has
    been trying to be better than other people."
If you accept the truth that we're all the same, and I'm the same
    as everybody else, the mind will give in, and align to the
    new way of acting.

We have individuality.
We are an individual perception of Self.
You can expand your individuality, until you embrace the
    universe, but You are still perceiving it.
Individuality is never lost.
We are always individual and universal at the same time.
Our mind can't accept that — being the microcosm and
    macrocosm simultaneously.

How can you be a human being and the whole of humanity —
  yet that is exactly what we are.

Challenge your concepts.
What is the way out of a prison?
1. Recognise that you are in one.
2. Design a prison — thus you're outside it.
If you recreate something, it disappears.
At the level of Self there is no karma.
Karma is only a belief system that keeps us from Self — it has a
  reality only in the level of mind.
Thinking sets up karma.
We can take charge of our thinking.
With a contextual creation everything works.
Do it often and make a habit of it.

A lot of what people call nirvana is unconsciousness.
If you lose your alertness, that's nothing.
Unless you're conscious, what's the point?
To me it is ever-expanding, ever-enriching, ever-brightening
  individual consciousness.
That does not mean individual consciousness, separate from all
  other-consciousness.
There is no separation, but there is no disappearance in
  consciousness.
The Buddha never disappeared — he was very aware, very alert,
  and was perceiving.
There is a lot of belief that there is some sort of altruistic state
  where we disappear.
I say that if you disappear yourself, and are no longer aware,
  you're in unconsciousness.
That is not total awareness, ultimate bliss, but *un* consciousness!
The more I become aware, even when sleeping, the more I
  expand my ability to be *conscious*.
Consciousness *is*, so it doesn't leave anything (like the body).
It depends where you look, but consciousness is, and "body"
  comes and goes.

Consciousness moves *in* the space, but not from it.
I don't get *out of* my body, separate myself — I'm whole.
I AM. I merely expand my awareness of this.
Body doesn't alter my Being. I am *being* body.

If you're coming from the space, from the centre of Being, you
   don't really need to engage in mental systems.
A mental system won't get you anywhere, since you're already
   There.
The thing is to unshackle the beliefs that are stopping you from
   fully realising your freedom.
It is really coming from the other end.
We don't want another system.
Systems don't work.
When I'm *THERE* I can use what system I like.
But a mental system cannot help me to *get* somewhere.

We have to decide what it is that we are.
If we are free beings and what we want is joy, love and peace,
   then what has it got to do with being intellectual?
Nothing!
Intellect is wonderful for communicating, for enjoying life in
   dissertation, and argument.
But it has nothing to do with freedom.
Recognise the mind for what it is.
The step to take is from being *in* the mind to, being the *observer*
   of mind.
I observe the thoughts that I have, and know that of themselves
   they are not the solution.

Science, theology and religion are all using mind to try and
   understand and explain God.
They are looking in the wrong place — looking in the ground to
   see why a flower blooms.
They are looking in the "formed" to discover how it *got*
   formed, or what forms it.

120

If I look at a chair to try to understand consciousness, I
    wouldn't get very far.
The wood and the legs tell me nothing about the man who
    made it.
Science looks at the formed to try to explain the unformed.
Medicine looks at disease to try and explain health.
We can't explain the outside world unless we study mind.
If we study mind, we can understand how our life is, why it is
    the way it is.

Creativity flows much better when we get the intellect out of the
    way.
Everything in life is useful and necessary, when used the right
    way.
You don't put a horse on your back, and start running over the
    jumps.
Just so with the mind.
You don't ask your mind to run your life for you.
You give the mind directions, and then it becomes a good
    servant.
Don't study form — study consciousness and mind, they tell
    you more.

Nothing happens that wasn't *thought*.
To think that nature is the ultimate law would be a fallacy — it
    is just the law that we allow now.
But that could change.
Science is discovering that the results of their experiments
    depend on their state of consciousness.
This has put a number of findings in doubt.
It is very difficult to make a pure experiment, as very often
    people find what they expect to find.
The purpose of observing a plant in spring, to me, would be to
    recognise myself.
To see the beauty and wonder of myself, the joy and scent.
To be the flower, and enjoy that expression of myself, is
    wonderful.

121

If I observe it like a scientist, I lose it — it becomes a "thing".
Science misses *the experiences* the joy of it.
Science must explore consciousness.

Look from the Centre, Allness, Oneness; if you see any twoness
    you smell a rat.
This is the context which destroys all myths.
If something shrinks your space or contains your freedom, see it
    for the robber it is.
The subconscious is like a photographic plate.
Whatever we imprint on it becomes our habit until we
    change it.
Make contextual creation a habit.
To "be free" is to acknowledge your freedom.
Also acknowledge that the other person is free.
Recognise that you are already God — and that all the others
    are too.
Relate to the Oneness of others.
Raise them to their Oneness, don't waste time on therapies.
If you give up all your concepts of god, you will discover It,
    because concepts are mental, and God is not in the mind.
This thought shocks people.
It is shocking to realise that all our thoughts, opinions, concepts
    and beliefs about who we are, and what "should" be done
    in the world, make no difference in the evolution of the
    planet. They have no value in the realm of Being.
It is also a great relief!

IT ALONE IS